4/27/48   207/275

Anton F. Pearson

Jeremiah For Today

JEREMIAH
FOR TODAY

by

Harry F. Baughman

MUHLENBERG
PRESS

The Muhlenberg Press • Philadelphia

Printed in U. S. A.

Contents

Foreword

"Preaching From Jeremiah" is the title of the graduate course in Gettysburg Seminary from which this volume grew. The purpose of the course is to explore the homiletical resources of this unique prophet's work. It is the author's conviction that any portion of Scripture yields its preaching values in richest measure to the student who succeeds most effectively in putting himself into the experience that produced the Scripture. Preaching is more than singling out a striking text which furnishes a point of departure for the presentation of the preacher's ideas. It is, or ought to be, the hospitality of the "House of Interpreter."

Interpretation is the chief business of the man in the pulpit. He is appointed to interpret God's word to man. He is an interpreter also of life. To employ the Scriptures with this twofold end in view requires much research which does not always appear directly in the sermon, but which, if it is properly done, makes the sermon.

One who embarks upon such background studies of Jeremiah promptly gains a positive impression. The prophet has convictions about a number of vital religious subjects. His revelation marks a distinct stage in the growth of man's understanding of God as it moves toward the full light of the New Testament. This revelation is not presented in a chapter-by-chapter sequence. Jeremiah's writings are not arranged in chronological order. But if one reads the book with an eye for the great themes on which the prophet speaks, one discerns the heart of his message.

This discovery led to the method pursued in the course, and reflected in the studies here presented. The Book of Jeremiah was studied patiently to discover what the prophet has to say—what God is saying through him—on such subjects as the nature of God, the fact of sin, the worship of God, the problem of suffering, the source of religious power. His passages bearing on these themes were assembled and classi-fied according to subjects. The contemporary quality of the prophet at once became apparent. He "came alive" for the student. He spoke to a living situation. He was "God's javelin."

In putting the notes of these lectures into book form, I have pursued the same method. Interpreting the message of the prophet, and interpreting life in terms of the message, have been the goal. Preaching values are suggested rather than outlined. Beneath it all is the design that the preacher in his use of the Bible shall not be fragmentary. "Read not little snatches of it here and there," wrote Woodrow Wilson in the Testaments given to soldiers. "Read great portions of it which shall be to you the road into the heart of its message." This volume aims to develop preaching which shall be "the road into the heart of the Bible's message."

Grateful recognition is given to those whose counsel and assistance have been invaluable in the preparation of these studies. I am especially indebted to my colleagues on the faculty of Gettysburg Seminary for helpful suggestions in the areas of their departments. Dr. Jacob Myers, Dr. Herbert Alleman, Dr. Carl Rasmussen, and Dr. Raymond Stamm have

viii

read portions of the manuscript and contributed wise counsel. I record with appreciation the services of typists who have assisted materially in the completion of the work, Mrs. George Thompson, now of Altadena, Calif., the Rev. Charles Aurand, of Hanover, Pa., and Miss Margaret Cook, of Gettysburg Seminary.

Frequent quotations are made from translations by John Skinner in *Prophecy and Religion* (Cambridge University Press, 1922) and by George Adam Smith in *Jeremiah*, The Baird Lecture, 1922 (George H. Doran Co.). The kind permission of The Macmillan Company and Harper & Brothers to make such quotations is much appreciated.

Jehovah-Hurled

THE MAN AND HIS TIMES

"Jerusalem that killeth the prophets and stoneth them that are sent unto her." Thus did Jesus characterize the religious and political capital of His nation. There is no record to indicate who were the prophets He saw as He spoke. One face, certainly, that must have come before Him was that of Jeremiah. For Jerusalem killed him with a death more cruel than execution and stoned him with a barrage more flinty than the rocks of her own field of stoning.

"Who being dead yet speaketh." Though he was "despised and rejected of men," branded in his time a failure and a traitor, and his voice silenced more than twenty-five centuries ago, Jeremiah yet speaks to this century with the accent of reality. His word for the political, social, and religious life of this day is as contemporary and relevant as though he now walked the streets of London, Washington, Berlin, or Moscow.

To mark the accents of his speech, to discern his insights, to note his perceptions of religious truth and duty, and their import for the life of our own day, is the purpose of this volume. This purpose can be best achieved by first tracing the career of the prophet and placing it in its proper historical setting, especially with reference to world movements.

1

Our knowledge of Jeremiah comes almost wholly from the book that bears his name. But the nature of this book is such that we actually have a very faithful picture, not only of his career and the external history of his period, but of his own life, his mode of thought, and his inner experiences. The book, upon its own testimony and internal evidence, is a compilation of Jeremiah's preaching and poetry, of his scribe Baruch's memoirs, and certain additions. All this material has been edited and in part assembled without necessary regard to chronological order or thought sequence.

Although it is not possible to start with Chapter 1 and trace in succeeding chapters the order of events, or even the sequence of messages in Jeremiah's career, students of the prophet's work have been able to classify with a reasonable degree of accuracy, both as to period and authorship, the various sections of the book. Thus George Adam Smith[1] has analyzed the work in these divisions:

(1) Prologue: 1:4-19. The call, about 627-626 B.C.
(2) Oracles: Chaps. 2-35. Mostly Jeremiah's.
(3) Oracles on foreign nations: Chaps. 46-51. Probably not of Jeremiah's authorship.
(4) Episodes in Jeremiah's life from 608 onward under Jehoiakim and Zedekiah to the flight to Egypt. Chaps. 26, 36-45. Mostly Baruch's.
(5) Expansions and additions. Historical appendix. Chap 52. Cf. II Kings 24-25.

An understanding of the national and international situation of the day is requisite to any appreciation of Jeremiah's career, and the import, ancient and modern, of his message. The prophet himself records with exactness his own point in history. "The word of the Lord came in the days of Josiah,

---

[1] George Adam Smith, *Jeremiah*, The Baird Lecture for 1922. George H. Doran Co. Pp. 9-10.

the son of Amon, king of Judah, in the thirteenth year of his reign. It came also in the days of Jehoiakim, the son of Josiah, unto the end of the eleventh year of Zedekiah . . . . unto the carrying away of Jerusalem captive in the fifth month" (1: 1-3). This means that the prophet's call came to him about 627-626 B.C., and that his warfare, begun with that call about mid-term in Josiah's reign, continued through the reigns of the succeeding kings, Shallum (or Jehoahaz), Jehoiakim, Jehoiachin, and finally Zedekiah, whose sorry reign wrote the closing chapter of Judah's history.

The Political Situation

Nearly a hundred years earlier the Northern Kingdom had fallen. Isaiah, Hosea, and Amos had spoken in vain to the consciences of rulers and people. The processes of history marched on, leaving a record which, set in the light of prophetic utterance, might have furnished a saving admonition to Judah. For she was now caught in the swirl of rising and contending states, and threatened from both the North and the South.

Chief among the dominant powers, holding in their might the destiny of Jeremiah's nation, were Egypt and Babylon, with a temporary threat hovering over the North in the fierce power of the Scythians. Egypt, long regarded by the Jewish people as the world power to be appeased, was now beginning to fade. Her might was being challenged, briefly by the Scythians, but fatally by the Chaldeans.

Through the years the Hebrew people had developed a policy of turning for security to alliances with the most powerful of the surrounding states. An almost exact parallel to their prevailing practice is to be seen in the history of many modern European states. Power politics with all the scheming, undercover agreements, and duplicity of modern state-craft were played to the limit. Isaiah urgently warned the Northern Kingdom of the peril of this course. Hosea, too, denounced the wavering policy of the national leaders. Their warnings fell upon dull ears as the nation, committed fully to the way of appeasement, was drawn farther and farther down the road of subservience until the fatal coup was delivered.

This policy persisted also in Judah in spite of the warning example of her sister to the North. If Israel failed to perceive the wisdom of Isaiah's counsel, "in returning and rest shall ye be saved," Judah even more stubbornly shut her eyes to the truth. Long accustomed to think of Egypt as the unconquerable state, Judah's leaders persisted in looking to Memphis for security. There were however those who were not above making secret agreements with whatever nation seemed most likely to succeed to world power. The undercover pact is not at all a modern invention. It was extensively employed in both Israel and Judah, and always with disastrous results.

THE RELIGIOUS SITUATION

At the same time that these political forces were at work undermining the stability of the nation, the religious practices of the people were contributing to the decadence. Influenced by both the philosophy and the seductive rites of the pagan religions, the Hebrew people resorted to the deities and the ceremonies of their heathen neighbors. The deities were those that symbolized fertility. The ceremonies were accompanied by lascivious practices and prostitution on a grand scale. And the systems flourished, not only because of their sensuous appeal to the fleshly passions, but also because they created and conveyed the idea of fertility. Shrines for the practice

4

of the rites supposed to secure fertility and prosperity sprang up on every hilltop. And this is the curious thing that came to pass in Judah: the nation did not formally abandon the worship of Jahweh, but combined with His worship, in name, the forms and ceremonies of the pagan cults. The resultant moral and spiritual confusion conspired with the political defeatism to lead Judah, as Israel had earlier been led, on the path toward oblivion.

The disintegrating process was halted for a time by the reign and the reforms of King Josiah. The youthful monarch, associating the decadence of the nation with the moral and religious confusion, instituted certain sweeping reforms based upon the Book of Deuteronomy.

A record in II Kings, beginning at 22:3, tells the story of this reform in its origin and application. When Josiah sent money to Hilkiah the high priest to pay workmen employed in repairing the temple, the priest told Shaphan, his messenger, "I have found the book of the law in the house of Jehovah." The book, generally believed to contain chapters 12-26, and 28, of the present Deuteronomy, was delivered to Shaphan, the scribe, who read it to the king. Josiah was awakened by its message to a sense of personal and national shortcoming. After conferring with his advisers, and consulting through them the prophetess Huldah, he commanded that the book of the law be read to all the people, "And the king stood by the pillar, and made a covenant before Jehovah, to walk after Jehovah, and to keep his commandments, and his testimonies, and his statutes, with all his heart and all his soul, to confirm the words of this covenant that were written in this book: and all the people stood to the covenant" (II Kings 23:3).

At once measures were instituted to make the covenant

effective. Religious practice was purified. As far as was possible Josiah's reforms abolished and outlawed the shrines and images and ceremonies that paganism had insinuated into the life of Judah. He succeeded in unifying the religious life of the nation. Instead of the multitude of shrines scattered throughout the land, the temple at Jerusalem was established as the center of religious worship. The Deuteronomic Code was made the court of appeals, the source of authority in the moral and social life of the nation. The Ark of the Covenant, Israel's ancient symbol of the divine Presence, was restored to its central place. These reforms, affecting the most vital areas of the nation's life, halted for a time the tottering course of the state. But their salutary influence was short-lived. After the first ardor of their accomplishment passed, it began to be apparent that these reforms affected chiefly the externals of the people's life, and, with the death of Josiah, the fruits of his labors decayed.

Into this situation Jeremiah was thrust. Scholars have not agreed upon the meaning of his name. The most recent conclusion is that it means "May Jahweh exalt." Earlier scholarship suggests the meaning "Jahweh hurls" or "Jahweh shoots." There is a striking description of the prophet's personality and career in this title. He was literally hurled into the life of his nation, there to contend with forces too powerful for him yet unable actually to defeat him. In this struggle Jeremiah was destined to give to the ages testimony that is invaluable.

Jeremiah was born after 650 B.C., at Anathoth, about four miles from Jerusalem. Of a priestly family, he inherited, besides some material property, certain mental and spiritual qualities that flowered into a clear analytical mind, a poetic nature, and a deep religious spirit. These endowments were

6

crowned by a quality which gave to his ministry, as to that of few other men, the effect of reality. Jeremiah was wholly dedicated to his God, his mission, and his people. By nature he was timid and retiring. Yet his sense of mission and his surrendered will produced in him a certitude so marked that the word he proclaimed was in a profound sense the "Word of the Lord." When George Adam Smith says of him, "No prophet was ever more sure of his word, or less sure of himself," he puts his finger upon the most revealing paradox in a life filled with paradoxes. This is why he was uniquely the prophet of the Word.

To understand Jeremiah's warfare and the pertinence of his message it is necessary to see the plight of his nation through his eyes. Superficially, it is easy to say of prophets like Isaiah, Hosea, and Jeremiah that when they assail the political alliances they ignore the realities of the situation; and when they speak about returning to God they are speaking vague and sentimental generalities. It is true that both Israel and Judah were small weak nations surrounded by powerful and predatory states likely to devour them no matter what course they followed. Safety seemed to depend entirely upon allying themselves with the most powerful state. It is also true that well-meaning spokesmen of religion have at all periods of crisis talked blithely about the importance of getting back to God. "What this nation needs today is to return to God," "We must find God or face ruin," are phrases heard today. They scarcely bear analysis. They break down at the first question, "What do you mean by getting back to God?"

But the warfare of the prophets is not to be equated with this kind of vague idealism. Jeremiah saw the resort to the alliance both as a symptom and a cause. It was to him evidence of the nation's readiness to forsake its covenant with God, to cease to be peculiarly and dynamically the "people of God." And, furthermore, it produced within the life of the nation a spirit and attitude that resulted in weakness.

Some Americans seeing the battlefields of France after the first world war were impressed by the manner of a guide as he pointed to a farm which had been in one family for more than a hundred years. "Each generation," he said, "has seen it invaded, and always the invader has come from the same direction." "But that cannot happen again," he continued. "Have you heard of the fortifications our government is building at the frontier?" That was the group's introduction to the Maginot Line and to the state of mind it helped to create. Later, published photographs of the extended system of pillboxes, defense in depth, underground communications, and powerful armaments served to impress upon the mind the impregnability of France's defense. After the fall of Paris and the demonstration of the weakness of her superb system of forts much was heard in many nations concerning the "Maginot Line complex." Men meant to say that the very strength of a material reliance may breed complacency and result in a perilous neglect of spiritual strength. Manifestly the leaders, if not many of the people of France, settled comfortably back into the feeling that the "forts up on the frontier" would automatically provide safety, and little attention need be given to that interior buttressing which comes from unity of purpose, righteousness, and noble living. They forgot the real meaning and cost of "Liberty, Fraternity, and Equality." The trial of the hapless Pétain revealed the mistaken choices of an old man, once a hero to the nation. But it revealed even more clearly the venality, opportunism, greed, baseness, and corruption that festered behind the

8

"security" of the Maginot Line. The forts were worthless when the interior resources of personality were spent. And the type of mind that was likely to allow spiritual resources to languish was induced by the existence and fancied security of the forts.

Something like that Jeremiah saw happening to his nation. His calls—like those of Isaiah and Hosea—to forsake the alliance and seek the higher reliance upon God were not vague, sentimental appeals. The prophets were the realists of their day and saw with absolute clearness what was happening to the inner spiritual strength of their nation. They were aware of a "Maginot Line mind," which they knew as an "Egypt- or Assyria-pact mind." They saw the degeneration of the spiritual force that accompanied the lowered moral standards, and resulted from their life's departure from the ways of God. Pagan forms of worship translated themselves into greed, sensuality, social chasms, and all the vitiating practices that drained the true strength of a nation. Against all these things, of which the alliance was both the symptom and the cause, they contended with all their power.

Jeremiah came to the day when he was convinced that surrender to the foe and crushing defeat for his nation was the only path open to his people. But for a part of his career at least he was aware of that of which history holds many examples. A nation, in the only kind of world we know, forsaking its sources of inner strength is doomed. But there is an ultimately unconquerable quality of spiritual strength. It is significant that in her two modern periods of crisis France instinctively sought to summon and recapture the spirit which was incarnate in Joan of Arc. And that spirit had as its dominant element the faith that not numbers, not size or material strength, but reliance upon God, is the source of victory.

George Bernard Shaw, in his drama, *St. Joan*, puts a thrilling reply into the mouth of Joan as she answers the fear of Robert Baudricourt that the French soldiers are outnumbered by the British and therefore doomed to be defeated. "One thousand like me can stop them," she exclaims, utterly innocent of any conceit. "Ten like me can stop them with God on our side. Our soldiers are always beaten because they are fighting to save their skins. . . . . But I will fight to teach them that the will of God may be done in France." Jeremiah was fighting not to save his skin, or that of the nation, but that the will of God might be done in the land.

A modern example of the truth of the prophet's insight is to be seen in the recent history of Norway, whose spiritual quality and actual experience furnished the inspiration for John Steinbeck's *The Moon Is Down*. He pictures the physical, military subjugation of a people whose spiritual defeat the force of the invader cannot by any means encompass. Suffering, punishments, servitude can be imposed upon the occupied nation, but the most cherished fruit of victory, conquest of spirit, eludes the victors. Puzzled, baffled, themselves beaten within, they perform their duties without zest, and sometimes in sodden fear. One of the storm troopers ironically exclaims, "We have conquered them as the flies conquer the fly paper."

Turning from a fictional to an actual setting, one sees this very quality incarnate in a man like Bishop Berggrav, who could be imprisoned but not conquered, whose spirit was so dynamic that even behind bars he forced his Nazi captors to change his guards every fortnight lest they be converted by him. To that kind of spiritual strength Jeremiah sought to call his nation. The hope of accomplishment fired his earlier messages. The recognition of failure colored

10

and gave character to his later messages and activity. His warfare, both in its immediate impact upon the life and events of his own day and in its import for the life of any age, is to be understood in the light of this perception.

This warfare, Jeremiah's campaign, was developed within the framework of the changing national situation, which will be sketched in the succeeding chapter. In its essence it can fitly be described in the language of the letter to the Ephesians: "For our wrestling is not against flesh and blood, but against the principalities, against the powers, against the world rulers of this darkness, against the spiritual hosts of wickedness in the heavenly places" (Eph. 6:12).

The Warfare

Bring me my bow of burning gold!
Bring me my arrows of desire!
Bring me my spear! O clouds, unfold!
Bring me my chariot of fire!

I will not cease from mental fight,
Nor shall the sword rest in my hand,
Till we have built Jerusalem
In England's green and pleasant land.

—From "Milton," WILLIAM BLAKE.

Jeremiah's warfare was the "mental fight" to build the true Jerusalem. He would have builded it, or preserved it, in Judah. But when that Jerusalem could not be saved, and all his warfare to thwart the powers that were destroying it was unavailing, he refused to let the sword rest in his hand until what was necessary for building a better Jerusalem in every land was accomplished. His "wrestling was not against flesh and blood" merely, but against "spiritual hosts of wickedness." It took place in an arena whose features have been duplicated in every period of human history and to which the twentieth century furnishes many striking parallels. If the story of this warfare were read with an alert imagination by the rulers and leaders of the nations now contending for world domination, it could well determine the course of

12

modern history. It can be best interpreted by fitting it into the developing scene of which it was a part.

The Call and Early Oracles

The paradox of Jeremiah's timid hesitancy and bold certainty is apparent in his recital of the call.

Now the word of Jehovah came unto me saying, Before I formed thee in the belly I knew thee and before thou camest forth out of the womb I sanctified thee. I have appointed thee a prophet unto the nations. Then said I, Ah, Lord Jehovah, behold I know not how to speak; for I am as a child. But Jehovah said unto me, Say not, I am a child; for to whomsoever I shall send thee thou shalt go, and whatsoever I shall command thee, thou shalt speak. Be not afraid because of them; for I am with thee to deliver thee, saith Jehovah. Then Jehovah put forth his hand and touched my mouth, and Jehovah said unto me, Behold I have put my words in thy mouth: see, I have this day set thee over the nations and over the kingdoms, to pluck up and to break down, and to destroy, and to overthrow, to plant and to build (1:4-10).

With this call to which we shall give consideration under the theme, "Jeremiah and the Word of The Lord," began the prophet's warfare. Primarily it was a struggle to reclaim Judah to fellowship with and obedience to God. In that reality in religion, Jeremiah well knew, lay the only hope for the nation. But it was not quite so simple as that. There were battles within his major campaign. That which began as a simple, straightforward call to a clearly discerned and sharply defined duty became involved with many factors, and developed in various directions. Thus the Book of Jeremiah tells the story of a life struggling against diverse elements yet unified in its central purpose by its relation to God's will.

13

Reserved for more adequate consideration in later and appropriate chapters are the visions and parables that proved to be mediums through which the word of the Lord became Jeremiah's possession. In this brief survey of the prophet's career it is sufficient to note that God spoke to him through the common experiences of daily life, just as Jesus later imparted to men the deep truths of God's kingdom through pictures of the life of nature and human experience. Linked together in the narrative are Jeremiah's account of his call and the vision of the almond tree. This is significant. The sensitive young man of Anathoth, deeply concerned about the course and destiny of his nation, must have been brooding upon all that was transpiring and all that threatened the nation. In the midst of his reveries and perplexity his eyes fastened upon a budding almond tree. The almond tree was among the first to awaken in spring after the sleep of winter. Its Hebrew name *shaqed* was akin to the Hebrew word meaning "awake." Like Saul Kane in John Masefield's "Everlasting Mercy," looking at nature with new eyes after his conversion and hearing "the babbling brook speaking of paradise," Jeremiah saw the yearly phenomenon of nature with eyes open to behold her hidden truths. The budding almond tree was God speaking to him and saying that He was awake and "watching over His word to perform it." Afterward the prophet associated in his own mind this vision and the call of God to declare His word. It was a part of the process by which God made him captive that He might make him free. He was now committed irrevocably to a Cause. The Cause was the will and the word of the living God.

Closely associated in the narrative with these earlier revelations of God to the young prophet is his account of the boiling caldron (1:13, 14): "The word of the Lord came

14

to me the second time." Again Jeremiah saw in a common-place experience the movement of God. This time it was so ordinary an occurrence as a caldron boiling over a fire, and its bubbles were from the north. It could have been a touch of superstition, but Jeremiah saw in this, too, a significance. Trouble was brewing for his nation. Presently it would boil over. And to his discerning eye it was apparent that this disaster would boil out of the north.

Awakened now, Jeremiah began his struggle. His first messages announced a peril threatening from the north, now in his thinking quite manifestly identified with the Scythians. Later he was to revise this. But he perceived very clearly the real danger to the life of the nation within the nation itself. And to this his first messages were addressed. It is to be observed that his forward-looking quality was early mani-fested. Others, particularly the men about the king, looked toward Egypt. They were traditionalists, bound to the past. Because Egypt had been the power to be reckoned with, she must continue to be. Because their fathers had made pacts with Egypt, they must also look to the Nile. Jeremiah looked ahead and saw that the future was with the rising people to the north. These states with youthful vigor would replace the fading power of Egypt. Around this conflict in the inter-pretation of history no small part of the prophet's struggle revolved.

Jeremiah began his prophetic career at Anathoth about 626 B.C. To this period belong, in the main, Chapters 2:2–4:4. Here are found his earlier oracles in which he sought to call Judah back to reality in religion and to revive the positive fellowship with God in which he saw the only hope for the nation. The clear impression left by his writings of this period is that he cherished a belief in the possibility of reclaiming the nation and averting threatening disaster. His remonstrances were for people who had played the harlot, a figure of speech not only suggestive of the lascivious practices of the fertility cults, but descriptive of the faithlessness of the people to their God. Let them heed the call now to return to the God whom they had forsaken. Then they may hope to find pardon and deliverance.

From this time on and with increasing emphasis Jeremiah dwelt upon the theme of the shame of faithlessness. He painted the faithlessness of man against the background of God's faithfulness. This is the appeal of Chapter 2. God is faithful. In all His dealings with His people He has been true to His covenant. Integrity is the mark of God's creation. Nature is held together by it. Only yourselves are faithless. Upon this theme his message rings the changes. It is at the very heart of his conception of religious relationship.

Throughout all the preaching of this period there runs the urgent note of pleading, remonstrance, warning, but withal a consciousness of futility and failure. One cannot but mark, particularly because of its disclosure of Jeremiah's nature and its bearing upon his sense of call, the note of reluctance, doubt, and even disputatiousness toward God. The prophet embarks upon his mission under protest. He draws back from it and finally speaks only because God literally hurls him into the situation. He laments that he has been born. He suffers acute pain because of the burden and sin of his people, "My bowels, my bowels, O my pain," he exclaims in sharp agony. He feels called upon to forgo the satisfactions of home and family life. He even upbraids God, declaring that the Almighty has taken unfair advantage of him. All of this is preserved in poetry so beautiful and moving that we really do not know Jeremiah until his oracles have been translated in poetic form. He voices the cry of his doubt in exactly the same terms which distraught mankind has employed through all the years.

Righteous art thou, O Jehovah, when I contend with thee; yet would I reason the cause with thee. Wherefore doth the way of the wicked prosper? Wherefore are they all at ease that deal very treacherously? (12:1).

To this general period also belong Chapters 4:5—6:30, allowing that certain lines whose reference is to another situation have been included in the chapter and verse formation. Here the prophet uses the peril of the Scythian hordes to awaken his people, if possible, to the doom that threatens them if they turn not from their evil ways. His forecast of disaster is presented in language picturesque and stirring to the utmost degree. Always in these sections it is to be observed that the pronouncement of doom is conditional. "If thou wilt return, O Israel, saith Jehovah, if thou wilt return unto me and put away thine abominations out of my sight, then shalt thou not be removed" (4:1). The prophet sees the possibility of repentance and renewal.

The Period of Josiah's Reforms

AT ANATHOTH

In the year 621 began a movement of profound significance to the nation and to the career of Jeremiah. It was then that the Deuteronomic Code was discovered and made the basis of the sweeping reform movement whose aims have already been noted. We may believe that the materials of Chapters 7, 8:8, and 11, with some possible exceptions, belong to the early days of Josiah's reform, which Jeremiah welcomed. Some commentators question his approval of it, but

17

it is generally conceded that the young prophet approved the goals of the reformation movement and threw his influence and energy into the cause.

It is reasonable to suppose that Jeremiah, by his espousal of these reforms as well as by his denunciations of his people's sins, aroused the enmity of his neighbors and kinsfolk. Especially was he likely to incur the wrath of the priestly group and all those who derived influence and profit from the many shrines which Josiah's reforms abolished. He began to experience that which Jesus was later to describe: "A prophet is not without honor save in his own country and in his own house" (Matt. 13:57). The hostility of Jeremiah's townfolks culminated in a plot against his life (11:18 ff).

This plot—which incidentally brought out the human, vindictive quality of Jeremiah and revealed him to be far from a meek "suffering servant"—became a second point of departure in his career. Beaten, discouraged, ready to give over the struggle, he retired to the sidelines, there to sulk and protest to God. Other men of God had similar experiences when, because they could not see the whole of God's plan, they succumbed to despair. Elijah in the reaction after his contest with the priests of Baal retired to his cave and yielded to the black mood of defeat: "The children of Israel have forsaken thy covenant, thrown down thine altars, and slain thy prophets with the sword: and I, even I only, am left: and they seek my life to take it away" (I Kings 19:10). Jonah, the reluctant missionary, preaching doom to the Ninevites for their sin, became a disappointed preacher because his message was effective. He had no place in his religious thinking for the possibility of repentance and salvation for gentiles and pagans. His vision did not sweep God's horizons. And when the people of Nineveh from the king down repented and found mercy, Jonah, supposing his prophecy was not vindicated, retired to sulk in the shade of a gourd. John the Baptist, who once declared so confidently of Jesus, "Behold the Lamb of God that taketh away the sins of the world," yielded to the mood of doubt. Languishing in prison, he sent messengers to Jesus asking: "Art thou he that should come, or look we for another?" So did Jeremiah succumb to black thoughts and the spirit of defeat when some of his predictions were not fulfilled and the men of Anathoth plotted against his life.

But God would not let him alone. He was preparing to lift him above his own mood. To the sulking, defeated prophet He said, "If thou hast run with footmen and they have wearied thee, then how canst thou contend with horses?" (12:5).

"Wearied by amateurs," might well be the modern interpretation of God's sermon to Jeremiah, and through him to all discouraged, defeated souls. What is God's answer to the prophet's mood of despair? He gives him a bigger, more challenging task. If he has been wearied by amateurs, God will now thrust him into the contest with professionals. Many a man has found himself by losing himself in a greater task. The outcome of Jeremiah's reverie was to move him on to Jerusalem, away from the village of Anathoth and contending with footmen, into the city and the contest with horses.

IN JERUSALEM

Thus Jeremiah moved—literally "God-hurled"—into the second phase of his warfare. He went to Jerusalem and there his enlightenment really began. He expected to find in that center—the seat of the temple, the home of the priests, the place of the king—all the best fruits of the reform. Disappointment was his first experience. The disappointment grew into disillusionment. To this dawning, growing feeling a poem included in Chapter 5 testifies eloquently:

> Run to and fro
> Range ye the streets of Jerusalem,
> Look now and know,
> And search her broad places,
> If a man ye can find—
> If there be that does justice
> Aiming at honesty.
> (That I may forgive them).
> Though they say "As God liveth,"
> Falsely they swear.
> Lord are thine eyes upon lies?
> And not on the truth?
> Thou hast smitten, they ail not,
> Consumed them, they take not correction.
> Their faces set harder than rock
> They refuse to return.
> But I said "Ah they are the poor
> And therefore the foolish!
> They know not the way of the Lord,
> The Rule of their God.
> To the great I will get me,
> With them let me speak.
> For they know the Way of the Lord,
> And the Rule of their God:
> Ah, together they have broken the yoke,
> They have burst the thongs."
>
> —5:1-5; tr. by George Adam Smith

Steadily the prophet's disillusionment grew. (Note 9:11, 6:16-20, 8:4-8.) Jeremiah's clear vision enabled him to see the external, legalistic, formal quality of that which was the end product of the reform. With greater zeal and intensity

20

he now carried forward his struggle, all the while accumulating a complexity of antagonisms, but at the same time acquiring an increasing perception of the reality—the inwardness—of the religion of the spirit. He kept his eye on the one goal. Step by step he progressed to the final knowledge that even the once-cherished, beloved forms must go in order that true religion—the life of fellowship with God—may be recovered. Here began that growing awareness of the evils of trust in institution, code, ritual, without the spirit. Jeremiah's most vital truths were preached "in the wake of the reform," a fact whose significance will be considered in the chapter "Jeremiah and Religious Dynamic."

The final crushing blow to any hope the prophet cherished of recovering the way of the Lord came with the death of Josiah in the battle of Megiddo in 608. And with the defeat of this hope there began a third and more intricate phase of Jeremiah's struggle.

THE PERIOD OF DISINTEGRATION

SHALLUM OR JEHOAHAZ

Josiah was succeeded by his son Shallum whose reign was brief indeed, a scant three months. Judah, after the defeat at Megiddo, was now really a pawn in the hands of Necho of Egypt, to whom Shallum was not acceptable. The monarch summoned the hapless ruler to Egypt, whence he never returned. Jeremiah celebrates this with his lines (22:10), "Weep not for the dead, neither bemoan him, but weep sore for him that goeth away: for he shall return no more nor see his native country"—a prediction that was fulfilled.

In the place of Shallum, Necho elevated to the throne another son of Josiah, Eliakim, to whom was given the name Jehoiakim. This move was parallel to the modern practice which conquering states employ, of establishing puppet rulers in subdued territories. Jehoiakim could be depended upon to serve the interests of the Egyptian overlord.

JEHOIAKIM

Judah was now subject to Egypt and her ruler and leaders were convinced that the future was with this southern power. Accordingly they trimmed their policies in that direction. But Jeremiah perceived that the future was with the rising power to the north, not any longer Scythia, but Babylon. And it was this conviction, together with the deepening perception of the rigid quality of Judah's sin: "The sin of Judah is writ with a pen of iron and with the point of a diamond; it is graven upon the tablet of their hearts" (17:1), that determined the unwavering course the prophet thenceforward pursued. He knew that Judah must be captured, the framework of her institutions destroyed, all her pride crushed, in order that pure religion might ultimately be preserved. And to that end he directed his struggle even though it meant shame, personal disgrace, loss, and apparent defeat.

The ruling house of Italy, the House of Savoy, was thrown out of power by popular choice in June, 1946. Strong leaders had been followed by a succession of weaker kings until finally the House of Savoy could no longer be tolerated in Italy. As this denouement approached, King Humbert, surrounded by dilettante princes and nobles and heeding their counsel, refused to see the menacing doom. Traditionalists to the end, they clung to a dream of power that had already evaporated. The king and his mistaken yes men finally were compelled to retire into exile amid shame and derision.

Jerusalem and the house of Judah in 608 were exactly like that. Jehoiakim was surrounded by a court whose eyes

22

were turned toward the past and whose ears were closed to every warning of approaching doom. Jeremiah was the realist facing the present and looking into the future. And his was the voice—unheeded—that was persistently lifted on behalf of the things that could stay the disaster.

He is authority for the statement that at the beginning of the reign of Jehoiakim he was commanded by the Lord to stand at the gate of the temple and call upon the nation, presumably through its leaders, to repent, and to announce doom if it refused to hear the voice of the Lord (chap. 26, also 7:3-15, 21-23). This forthright message denouncing dead trust in temple forms and ritual and delivered in the very gate of the temple, served to crystallize the opposition. The Formalists bitterly assailed him. Yet Jeremiah reiterated his message. One thinks of Luther saying, as he was warned not to go to the Diet at Worms, "I will go though there be as many devils aiming at me as there are tiles on the roofs." One thinks of Queen Esther's sublime courage. "I will go in unto the king, which is not according to the law: and if I perish, I perish" (Esther 4:16). Or one thinks of Peter confronting the Sanhedrin with his challenge, "Whether it is nobler to obey God rather than men, judge ye."

The story of the prophet's conflict now becomes vivid, and indeed contemporary. He relates how the conviction came to him that he must preserve the oracles and messages that were the word of the Lord through him to the nation. Baruch was employed as his scribe. In the fourth year of Jehoiakim's reign, that is, 604, or twenty-three years after his own call, this work of committing the word to parchment was begun. The defeat of Necho in the battle of Carchemish, just before this time, has been suggested as the reason for Jeremiah's conviction that the messages must be given permanent form. It was a laborious task which required more than a year of painstaking effort. The scroll was finally read. Jeremiah was in prison at the time, and Baruch read it to the people gathered in the house of Gemariah, the son of Shaphan (36:10). The outcome of this reading was that Baruch was commanded to have the scroll read to the king. And here (36:11-19) is one of the most dramatic pictures in the book. As Jehudi read the scroll, the arrogant Jehoiakim listened, seated before a fire in the winter palace, making no attempt to conceal his scorn. When two or three leaves were read, the king, taking out his penknife, cut them into shreds and contemptuously cast them into the fire that burned in the brazier before him. Here again one cannot fail to see the counterpart of the modern burnings, for example by the Nazis, of unwanted literature. Reading the sequel to this and the modern versions, one cannot but hear a solemn hymn resounding, "The Word they still shall let remain, nor any thanks have for it."

Then began a new work of committing the oracles to parchment. Now Jeremiah's battle became more distinct. It had started in Anathoth with the call to repent and return, warning the people of the peril that threatened from the north. It had then moved on to Jerusalem, where it became involved with priests and institutions. Now the prophet was hurled into conflict with the king and the men who surrounded him. Some of these courtiers, princes, laymen were of finer quality and impulse than the king, and at least once Jeremiah, recognizing this superiority, appealed over the heads of the priests and princes to the "laymen" (19:1). But those upon whom Jehoiakim chiefly relied were men who had guessed wrong, whose faces were set in the wrong direction, whose self-interest dictated the preservation of the status quo. Throughout the entire reign of this craven king, Jeremiah's voice was unwavering. His perception was clear, both in matters of religion and statecraft. The deadness and corruption of the nation steadily forced him to the settled conviction that Judah must be completely broken and refashioned. To this conviction the parable of the potter's vessel, whose interpretation is considered in a later chapter, contributed materially. It is important, however, to note the fact of this conviction in Jeremiah's total outlook. For it is the basis of the counsel consistently offered later to surrender to the Chaldeans.

A measure of confirmation was given to the prophet's contention by the result of the battle of Carchemish in 605. Necho was defeated. The power of Egypt was broken. And Babylon was established as a world power. Shortly after this Jehoiakim died. Chapter 17:11 gives Jeremiah's estimate of his reign: "As a partridge that sitteth on eggs which she hath not laid, so is he that getteth riches and not by right. In the midst of his days they shall leave him. And at his end he shall be a fool." And in 22:13-19, after reciting the king's record of injustices and oppressions, he concludes his message: "They shall not lament him, saying 'Ah my brother,' or 'Ah sister!' They shall not lament for him saying, 'Ah his glory!' He shall be buried with the burial of an ass, drawn and cast forth beyond the gates of Jerusalem." The end of Jehoiakim did not fulfill this description literally. He did die at the age of thirty-six, unwept, unhonored, and unsung.

JEHOIACHIN

Events began now to move toward a climax. Jehoiakim was succeeded by Jehoiachin, a mere youth, whose reign covered the brief space of three months when disaster finally overtook Judah. He had inherited a hopeless situation, coming to the throne with the Chaldean army literally at the gates of the city. Nebuchadnezzar led his armies to the first conquest of Jerusalem carrying the king and many of the people into captivity "by the waters of Babylon."

In all these events Jeremiah played the role of participant and not merely spectator or commentator. While it is impossible to assign with exactness each of the prophet's utterances, it is possible to discern the development of his convictions. He was sadly aware of the cravenness of the majority of the leaders. He became increasingly convinced of the essential dishonesty of great masses of the people. From his first experiences in Jerusalem when he sought in vain through the market places for an honest man, he carried a profound distrust of the moral quality of the nation. He strove by preaching, warning, and poetic composition to stem the tide of infidelity. Typical of his efforts is the incident of his appeal to the Rechabites. Chapter 35, usually employed as a lesson in temperance, is really a stirring call to integrity. The abstinence from wine practiced by the Rechabites was only one item of their discipline. Jeremiah summoned them chiefly to be to the nation an example of fidelity to a way of life commanded by the fathers. While others were turning aside and following false gods and pursuing undisciplined ways, these sturdy sons of Rechab were standing firmly upon the established principles of their house, retaining their distinct character: the salt, so to speak, preserving its savor.

"There stand the Rechabites," Jeremiah was saying to the nation. "Recover their stability and integrity and you shall find life." This incident during the reign of Jehoiakim serves to reveal a phase of the prophet's struggle against the nation's decadence, and to show how the conviction was growing

26

within him that a hopeless lack of integrity was possessing the people and their leaders.

The old religious practices, abolished by Josiah's reforms, persistently raised their heads. The idea back of them would not die. Religion is a device to produce prosperity. When disaster threatened after the reform had banished the shrines, there were repeated revivals of the superstitious beliefs and practices of the fertility cults. Against these tendencies creeping into the life of the nation from various sources Jeremiah stubbornly contended. His struggle was compelling him to strike out in new directions.

As the prophet watched the situation grow steadily worse he came finally to the fixed conclusion that there was but one way of recovering the true spiritual life for which the Hebrew people were originally destined. Judah must be crushed. The old familiar forms and reliances must go. And Jeremiah saw the Chaldeans as the instrument for the accomplishment of this purpose. To this conclusion can be traced what seems like the defeatist, traitorous counsel and behavior of the prophet throughout the last days of the nation. He counseled surrender to the armies of Nebuchadnezzar. The leaders leveled the same charges at him that military men have always hurled at those who oppose their ends. "He weakens the hands of the men of war." "Have this fellow put to death; he takes the heart out of all the citizens and soldiers" (38:4—Moffatt). But Jeremiah counseled surrender not as a fifth columnist, or collaborator, but because he was sweeping far horizons and visualizing the eternal purposes of God.

Doom began for Judah in 597 with the siege and first capture of Jerusalem. Jehoiachin was carried a prisoner to Babylon. With him went a part of the population, the most skilled elements, while the remnant, the less competent, were left to continue their life about Jerusalem. With these Jeremiah remained, and for a time, paradoxically, wrote the most hopeful of his poems.

ZEDEKIAH

Nebuchadnezzar, after the first deportation, set a puppet king, Zedekiah, to rule over the remnant at Jerusalem. Unfortunately for the best life of this colony, the old, cunning, reactionary group surrounded him. These backward-looking counselors, still tying Judah's fortunes to the now waning power of Egypt, precipitated the final death blow to the nation by encouraging and joining the tribes revolting against the Chaldean rule. This brought the army of the Babylonian king to the gates of Jerusalem in the second siege of the city in 586. The record of the siege is in the Book of Jeremiah, Chapters 21, 32-34, 37, and 38.

During the siege of the city Jeremiah's conflict rose to its most intense pitch. His counsel to surrender was reiterated against the promptings of all the king's advisers, including those prophets who claimed to speak in the name of Jehovah. Chief among these was Hananiah, whom Jeremiah denounced as a false prophet, ridiculing the trances and ecstasies in which Hananiah and his associates professed to receive revelations from God. Thus Jeremiah's warfare was given still another direction. He was in conflict with the spokesmen of his own religion.

The fortunes of Jeremiah sank lower and lower. At one time he was arrested and imprisoned because he was suspected of attempting to go over to the enemy. This grave charge was not sustained, but hatred and suspicion had fastened themselves upon him. Finally he was incarcerated in a cistern where his sad plight was discovered by a eunuch, who, with a humaneness not displayed by his superiors, rescued him. Yet he was not wholly without influence. For Zedekiah consulted him, and at times gave evidence of actually desiring to heed his counsel.

No power in Jerusalem was able to hold off the overwhelming forces of the enemy, and finally the city fell. Zedekiah met a miserable end. His sons were slain in his sight. His eyes were then put out and he was led into captivity, while his palace and the great houses of his nobles were put to the flames.

THE PERIOD OF CAPTIVITY

After the fall of Jerusalem and its wanton destruction, Gedaliah was made governor of the feeble colony remaining. Jeremiah continued in Jerusalem, sharing the lot of its disheartened inhabitants. Chapters 30, 31, 39-44 record the history of this period. It was marked chiefly by quarrels over the remains. Ishmael, a rebel, covetous of the paltry leadership, plotted against Gedaliah and assassinated him. He was opposed by Johanan, who sought to avenge the death of Gedaliah and accomplish a semblance of order among the disorganized people. It seemed to him that safety lay in flight to Egypt and he consulted Jeremiah concerning it. The prophet asked for ten days that he might seek counsel of his God. At the end of this period of prayer and brooding he announced that the word of the Lord had again come to him. Still his counsel was against the resort to Egypt.

Baruch has two records of this period that are most significant. Chapter 45 records Jeremiah's counsel to his faithful associate. "Seekest thou great things for thyself? seek them not." Whatever dreams the younger man might have had of a new life with at least some reward of honor and distinction must not be indulged. They would prove to be merely illusions. "Forget yourself," the prophet seems to say, "and all your personal ambitions. Lose yourself in, and with, your cause. Only so can your testimony be established."

When the leaders, bent upon going to Egypt, resisted the counsel of Jeremiah and stubbornly persisted in their course, the prophet resorted to another of his object lessons. He took stones and hid them in the brick work at the entrance of Pharaoh's palace (43:9). These stones imposed upon Pharaoh's house, he declared, were a prophecy of Nebuchadnezzar's ultimate victory over the Egyptians. On these stones, laid upon the palace would be built the throne of Nebuchadnezzar, and he would smite and destroy the Egyptians. Jeremiah's prophecy, extreme in its language, fierce in its prediction, is evidence of the intensity of his feeling against Egypt and his conviction that the future, at least the short-term future, was with Babylon.

Maintaining to the very end the conviction that was his, battling stubbornly for the truth that he knew, Jeremiah was forced—crowning irony of all—to go with his people into Egypt. There he ended his days still doing battle for the true and spiritual worship of the living God.

Jeremiah and the Word of the Lord

Jeremiah, in John Singer Sargent's frieze of "The Prophets," is clad in a white robe. The symbolism of this in the artist's intention arouses speculation. Does he suggest that this weeping figure is merely a spectator and lamenter, who has kept his garments white by nonparticipation in the troubled affairs of his people? Does he mean to convey the thought of the purifying processes of hard and bitter experiences? "These"—arrayed in white robes—"are they who have come through great tribulation." Does his symbolism suggest the white light of the clear illumination that came to this prophet? Is this spotless robe the badge of one upon whom the light of the knowledge of God has shone with great intensity?

One's mind lingers upon the last of these suggestions. For if anything can be regarded as Jeremiah's distinctive characteristic, it is his unique place as a transmitter of God's revelation. His career is inexplicable unless one takes into account the most pronounced feature of the only record we have of it. Like the theme of a concerto, recurring throughout the work and binding its several parts together to give meaning to the whole, is the repeated theme of Jeremiah, "the word of the Lord came unto me." His career becomes intelligible in the light of that word. Jeremiah was not fighting his own battle. He was not applying his own wisdom to the problems of his people's life. He was not contending in his own strength against principalities or powers and the world rulers of darkness. He was not bringing the best wisdom, morality, judgment and skill of which he was capable to the building of his "beloved community." He had put on the whole armor of God, and was battling with the sword of the Spirit which is the word of God. He was bringing to bear upon the life of his day that which a later servant of God was destined to describe as "living and active, sharper than any two-edged sword, piercing even to the dividing of soul and spirit, and quick to discern the thoughts and intents of the heart" (Heb. 4:12).

Jeremiah is pre-eminently the prophet of the word. From the start of his career he was manifestly conscious of being guided by a will not his own. He was sure not only that he had been called to declare the word of the Lord, but that he had been predestined to this mission from before his birth. The intimation of this is especially clear in John Skinner's translation of the prophet's call (1:4-10):

There came to me this word of Jahwe
Before I formed thee in the womb I knew thee,
And before thou camest forth I set thee apart:
A prophet to the nations I ordained thee. . . . .
For to whomsoever I send thee thou shalt go.
And whatsoever I command thee, that thou shalt speak. . . . .
Then Jahwe stretched forth his hand and laid it on my mouth
    and said:
Lo I put My Word in thy mouth;
See I put thee in charge this day
Over the nations and kingdoms
To pluck up and pull down, to build and to plant.

This sense of destiny guided his entire career. Not merely the repetition of the phrase—it occurs more than a hundred times—but the decisions, the behavior, the reliances of the prophet, and the history of which he was an integral part, suggest the important bearing of his work upon our concept of inspiration. To be sure, one may not expect to find in the Book of Jeremiah a total Christian doctrine of the word. This chapter will be held within the limits of the theme "Jeremiah and the Word of the Lord." But one should discern in the experience of the prophet, and in the record of it, that which contributes materially to an understanding of how the will of God is apprehended by and channeled through an individual, and so applied to life that it is the very word of the Lord.

THE MAN WHO WAS INSPIRED

It is not necessary for us to read into the record much, if any, conjecture of our own. We need not be subjective in order to arrive at a reasonably clear understanding of the inspiration of at least this one spokesman of God. Certain deductions from and extensions of the testimony may with validity be made, especially when we come to consider the question, "How to the singer comes the song?" But the truth is that Jeremiah has so completely laid bare his own soul that the record which he has left becomes testimony, clear and direct, to the ways in which God makes known His will to an individual, and uses his capacities to communicate this to men as living truth.

A MAN POSSESSED BY GOD

Looking at the record of the book, then, as testimony, the first conclusion warranted by the evidence is that Jeremiah believed himself to be laid hold upon by God. His own

33

words leave us under no doubt that he felt himself to be a "man possessed by God." This is apparent in his reaction to his call. God had taken the initiative before he had conscious existence and was using forces within His grasp and power to shape him for the divinely chosen destiny. When the youth, under conviction, protested, "I am too young," God overcame his protestations. What were youth and inexperience? It was not the youth who was to speak. God would speak through him. He would make of him that which he could not of himself ever become—a fortified city, an iron pillar, brazen walls.

It is more vividly apparent as with his unfolding career he encounters the hostility of his closest friends, and, plunged into the slough of despair, upbraids God himself.

> Thou hast deceived me, Jahwe; and I was deceived:
> Wast stronger than I, and prevailedst.
> I am a laughing stock all the day:
> All men deride me.
> Whenc'er I speak I am mocked;
> Of violence and wrong is my cry;
> For Jahwe's word is to me a reproach
> And derision all day long.
> If I said I will seek to forget Him,
> And speak no more in His name,
> 'Twas like a glowing fire in my breast,
> Shut up in my bones.
> I was weary with keeping it under;
> I could not hold out.
> —20:7-9; tr. by John Skinner

The prophet speaks not because he has chosen to speak, but because he has been chosen. He preaches not because he is eager to deliver a message wrought out in the best counsels of his own mind, but because a Power he cannot resist, a

34

Power stronger than himself, has laid hold upon him. Though he would restrain his voice the divine compulsion operates and the truth can no longer be held back. Like a fire it burns and finally bursts forth.

In some of his most poignant psalms he pours forth the reluctance of his spirit to bear the unwanted testimony. Picturesquely he voices his lament.

> Cursed be the day I was born,
> The day when my mother bore me.
> Be it unblessed!
> Cursed be the man who brought to my father
> The good news, a man child is born.
> Making him glad!
> May that day be like the cities
> That God overthrew
> And pitied them not!
> May its morning hear the cry of distress,
> Its noon the shout of battle!
> Because it slew me not in the womb,
> That my mother had been my grave,
> And her womb pregnant forever.
> Why came I forth from the womb
> To see trouble and sorrow
> To consume my days in shame?
>
> —20:14-18; tr. by John Skinner

If he could have chosen his career, if at any time he could have relinquished it, how eagerly would he have done so. But he could not. God was too powerful.

This sense of the inevitability of the message—the sense of being driven by a compulsion that comes from beyond yet is within, is vital to an understanding of the prophet's steadfast refusal to deviate from the unpleasant and unwanted truth. He *must* proclaim the message though the proclamation strip him of friends and reputation, though it arm his enemies and destroy Judah. There is no choice. Like a Reformer following him by centuries, he seems to say, "Here I stand, I cannot do otherwise."

A survey of the passages confirming this truth would include the most dramatic scenes and oracles of his career. It would include his temple sermon (chap. 26); the preparation and reading of the scroll, first in the temple, then to King Jehoiakim (chap. 36); his persistent prophecies of disaster against the "comfortable" speeches of the false prophets (chaps. 23, 28, 29). It would include his counsel—traitorous in the eyes of his countrymen—to surrender to the Chaldeans (chap. 38, especially vss. 15, 16). He is not flattered by the confidence of the king, nor overcome by the fear of his displeasure. He speaks the distasteful truth and scorns the consequences.

We can examine only one of these—the temple sermon. The twenty-sixth chapter records an act which the priest's son of Anathoth, this timid, sensitive, young poet, could not of himself have done. And the record is in language that leaves us in no doubt about the compulsion under which the prophet acted.

Thus saith Jehovah, stand in the court of Jehovah's house and speak to all the cities of Judah . . . . all the words that I command thee unto them. Diminish not a word. It may be they will hearken and turn every man from his evil way. . . . . And thou shalt say unto them, thus saith Jehovah: if ye will not hearken unto me, to walk in my law which I have set before you, to hearken unto the voices of my servants the prophets, whom I send unto you . . . . then will I make this house (the temple) like Shiloh and will make this city a curse to all the nations on earth. And the priests and the prophets and all the people heard Jeremiah speaking these words in the temple (26:2-7).

36

When the storm of angry protest—by professional religionists who could not bear the thought of destruction of their sacred place and privileges, and by prophets and people who could not stand the uncomfortable truth—rose and swirled about him, the prophet made his calm reply. It was the same stubborn speech.

Now therefore amend your ways and your doings and obey the voice of Jehovah your God. . . . . But as for me, behold I am in your hands, do with me as is good and right in your eyes. Only know ye for certain, if ye put me to death ye will bring innocent blood upon yourselves and upon this city, for of a truth Jehovah hath sent me unto you to speak all these words in your ears (26:13-15).

A modern counterpart of that scene is the unforgettable picture of one who has visited Holyrood Castle, in Edinburgh, and later the humble home of John Knox. In the castle the visitor can readily picture the man of God facing the worldly, pleasure-loving courtiers of the queen and fearlessly denouncing their sins of the flesh while they listen contemptuously. Then the visitor makes his way to the house of the preacher and there upon the mantel sees inscribed these words that tell the story of a soul's drive and strength: "I am in the place required of my conscience to speak the truth, and therefore the truth I speak. Impugn it who list."

"Preaching," says Karl Barth, "is an act of daring, and only the man who would rather not preach and cannot escape from it ought ever attempt it." Jeremiah leaves as his first and strongest impression upon the reader that of a man who would rather not preach but cannot escape from it. "Thou hast persuaded me and I was persuaded. Thou art stronger than I, and hast prevailed."

The second conclusion warranted by the evidence of Jeremiah's testimony is that the prophet is manifestly a man who is in full possession of his faculties. His warfare brought him into sharp conflict with the false prophets, and out of his controversies with these seers and soothsayers came some of his most impassioned speeches which give us a further insight into the quality of his perception of the word of the Lord.

Jeremiah was not the only man in Judah who professed to speak in the name of the Lord or to have access to the counsels of the Eternal. There were others whose speech was delivered with equal certainty, in the same religious language, with fervency, eloquence, and power; and whose deliverances, moreover, were clothed with a certain accepted regularity of credentials and behavior that were presumed to validate them in the eyes of the people. One common procedure among these professional prophets was to enhance the plausibility of the supernatural source of their oracles and divinations by entering into a trance. They patently yielded possession of their faculties and announced as true revelation of the Divine that which came to them in their dreams and visions.

Against the background of these prophets Jeremiah's conception of a soul's access to God and his fidelity to His revelation is made to stand out in sharp relief. He has complete scorn for the dream, the trance, the ecstasy. He professes to see the truth of God with eyes that are open. And in this he makes a distinct contribution to our understanding of the word of the Lord.

Jeremiah's most severe indictment of the false prophets is that they are not capable of healing the ills of the nation because they are sharing in the very sins that are threatening

ruin. They have disqualified themselves as spiritual judges
by beclouding, with their own sins, the instrument of discernment.

> Broken is my heart, within me.
> All my bones quiver!
> I am like a drunken man,
> Like one overcome by wine
> Before Jahwe and His glorious majesty.
> For with adulterers the land is filled;
> Their course is bad, their power not right.
> Yea both prophet and priest are profane.
> Even in My house I have found their wickedness.
>
> —23:9-11; tr. by John Skinner

In Samaria's prophets I saw unseemliness:
They prophesied by Baal and misled my people,
In Jerusalem's prophets I have seen a horror:
Adultery, walking in lies and strengthening the hand of evildoers.
They are all to me like Sodom and the inhabitants of Gomorrah.

> —23:13, 14; tr. by John Skinner

With perfect confidence the prophet affirms the authen-
ticity of his message as against the ravings of the false prophets because he knows his own moral nature to be in harmony
with the will of God. It is as though he says with Tennyson's
"Galahad":

> My good sword carves the casques of men;
> My tough lance thrusteth sure;
> My strength is as the strength of ten
> Because my heart is pure.

But it is not only the question of moral and spiritual fit-
ness that is involved in this conflict. The question is, and
very illuminatingly for our purpose, the means of perception.

39

The false prophets rely upon trances and dreams to commend and render plausible their communications. Jeremiah, by implication, professes to employ consciously all his faculties to see, not in one sharp flash as by magic, but soberly, clearly, faithfully, the whole will and purpose of God for His people.

> I have heard what the prophets say who preach in My Name,
> Falsely saying I have dreamed,
> I have dreamed, I have dreamed.
> Will the heart of the prophets turn who prophesy lies?
> And in their prophesying. . . . .
> The deceit of their hearts
> Who plan that My people forget My Name
> Through the dreams they tell.
>
> —23:25-27; tr. by George Adam Smith

There is one clear impression left by Jeremiah's impassioned speeches as he confronts the false prophets who speak comfortable things and shows his contempt for the dreams and divinations of the yes men of the morally bankrupt leaders who would "heal my people's hurts lightly." It is that he is sure of the word of the Lord because he has faced the issues with all his faculties alert. Recognizing the fact that Jeremiah speaks with the vivid imagery of a true poet, we can only see in the testimony of his verse the expression of a man who knows that he sees clearly because he looks with open eyes at life's scene.

This naturally raises the question, "How then are we to distinguish between the true and the false prophet?" How could Jehoiakim or Zedekiah, for example, be expected to know whether Jeremiah or Hananiah had the true word of the Lord?

The question becomes quite contemporary. In our own

day we have witnessed men of every rank putting forth claims to speak in the name of the Lord, to be the agents of God ordained to accomplish His purpose. From the radio evangelists to Adolf Hitler, from Huey Long to Kaiser Wilhelm men have ever advanced lofty claims. "On me as German emperor," said Wilhelm, "the Spirit of God has descended. I am His weapon, His sword, His vicegerent. Woe to the disobedient. Death to cowards and traitors." No less confident or blasphemous were the propaganda blarings of the braggart of Berchtesgaden. And every such claimant in his own place and to his own degree has been able to inspire confidence and fealty in some followers.

The perspective of history helps us to discern between the false claimant and the true. A historian after the event can write "Napoleon said there shall be no God. God said there shall be no Napoleon. And God always has the last word." But there is little solace or security for the dupes and victims of false leaders in the assurance that history will judge. The question persists, "How can we know the true prophet today?"

The only final criterion is that to which Jeremiah appealed. He first looked into the moral issues involved and into the moral life of the spokesman. He inquired into the self-interest of the prophet, and his eagerness to speak. All these measurements he applied as carefully as thoughtful men today may apply them. But his final criterion was that which is deeper than all these, yet correspondingly more difficult to define. He tested the word by truth. Does the prophet's word correspond to truth? The court of final appeal is not the flourish with which the claim is made, nor the trappings of mystery and occultism, nor even the success of the prophet's appeal, his popular acceptance. It is the self-authenticating quality of the word. The false prophets, with their "prosperity just around the corner" theme, proclaimed the message their employers and the thoughtless populace wanted to hear. Their messages did not match the truth. Said Jeremiah: "They prophesy lies."

"They speak a vision out of their own heart, and not out of the mouth of Jehovah" (23:16). "I have not sent these prophets yet they ran: I spake not unto them yet they prophesied" (23:21). Against this eagerness of the false prophets to speak Jeremiah set his own reluctance as evidence of the fidelity of his message to God's will. His speech contains a perpetual instruction concerning the call, the credentials, and the testimony of God's messengers. "I have not hastened from being a shepherd after thee; that which came out of my lips was before thy face" (17:16). His message, he means to say, is not that which he has desired to speak, but that which God has constrained him to speak.

Like Amos, challenged by the angry crowd, this man of God appealed to the word itself. Years before, speaking in the Northern Kingdom, a man who had "seen things steadily and seen them whole" sought to awaken the people to a sense of their sin. And when these people, who hated to face the unpleasant truth, demanded of him his credentials, he could appeal to no parchments, no school of the prophets, no ecclesiastical authority. He appealed to the word itself. It is its own evidence. "Shall two walk together except they have agreed? Will a lion roar in the forest if he have no prey?" See how the word matches the facts. "The Lord Jehovah hath spoken, who can but prophesy?" (Amos 3:3-8).

Jeremiah in even more sublime confidence makes the same appeal. Listen to his words in the twenty-third chapter:

42

The prophet that has a dream
Let him relate a dream;
And he that has my Word
Let him declare my Word in truth.
What has the chaff to do with the wheat
Is Jahwe's oracle.
Is not my Word like fire,
Like a hammer that shatters the rock?

—23:28, 29; tr. by John Skinner

How Did the Word of the Lord Come to Jeremiah?

A poem by Richard Watson Gilder which bears the title, "How to the Singer Comes the Song," describes the manner in which the common facts and experiences of life—the smell of the seas, the glittering sunlight upon the waves, the crimson sky at sunset, the throbbing hurt of sorrow—awaken the voice of the poet and set vibrating within his soul those chords that swell forth in his song.

This power of the common objects and experiences of daily life to stir up the prophetic and poetic genius of the prepared soul is one of the pronounced features of the testimony presented by Jeremiah's poetry. It is most impressive, and, considered in connection with some of the truths we have distilled from preceding passages, suggests a clue to the answer of the question that now arises. "How did the word of the Lord come to Jeremiah?"

THE PREPARATION

The prophet was aware that he did not stand alone in society. He was the product of influences and forces that had been working through long years to make him what he was. And in his account of his call he describes clearly a fact

43

of his own consciousness which bears definitely upon this
question:

> Before in the body I built thee,
>   I knew thee;
> Before thou wast forth of the womb
>   I had hallowed thee:
> And a prophet to the nations had set thee.
>
> —1:5; tr. by George Adam Smith.

Back of Jeremiah's perception of truth and duty were the
revelations and the records of them that God had made to
other spiritual geniuses. There were the declarations of
fundamental duty mediated through Moses. There was the
unfolding history of "this nation under God." There were
the records of great souls' communion with God and insights
into His nature. There was the preaching of men like Isaiah,
Amos, and Hosea. The message of Hosea, particularly, made
a profound impression upon Jeremiah. His influence is clearly
discernible in the later prophet's writings. And there were
those dispositions of mind and spirit which were the product
of an inheritance from generations of religious forebears. For
whatever misconceptions of nature and practice had crept
into the priestly group, the fact is that religion was in the
blood of Jeremiah's people. They were occupied with
religion. They were concerned with its interpretation and
application. They spoke of God and ordered their lives in
the light of His Being. This stream of religious influence
flowed to Jeremiah, and by all the laws of inheritance produced a nature sensitive to religion and capable of responding
to the stimulus that comes from beyond our bourne of time
and place. The deposit of generations was in the life of this
man, and shows itself in his declarations.

All of these elements, the total religious experience of the race, the records of other revelations, the ongoing stream of life with its deposits, contributed to the whole nature and capacity of Jeremiah to make him the kind of man who would perceive and respond to the word of the Lord. And his awareness of this preparation sings in his poetry: "Before thou wast forth of the womb I had hallowed thee."

THE PRAYER LIFE

We are greatly aided, furthermore, in our search for the answer to this question by the fact that the prophet's poetry is not only a record of history, but is a veritable photograph of his mental and spiritual processes.

Possibly the clearest, most direct light upon the question is that which is cast by the prophet's own devotional life, of which we have a most intimate record. In a collection of poetry which has been characterized as "The Confessions of Jeremiah" we have the record of a communion that was continued, intimate, and real. The prophet pours out his very soul as he carries to his God, whom he knows not merely as a national emblem, nor as a theological definition, but as a personal Companion, the most vital and perplexing problems of his life. "Righteous art thou, O Jehovah, when I contend with thee, yet would I reason the cause with thee: Wherefore doth the way of the wicked prosper? wherefore are all they at ease that deal very treacherously?" (12:1).

He brings the baffling question to God. He talks it out face to face. His prayers indicate that he knows God as One who is concerned about his every need. He is the *kind* of God to whom a man can take his problems. God is present, not a faraway Deity.

> Am I but a local God
> No far reaching God?
> Does a man hide in secret
> And I not see him?
> Is it not the heavens and earth
> I do fill?

—23:23-24; tr. by T. Crouther Gordon in *The Rebel Prophet*

Heal me, O Jehovah, and I shall be healed. Save me and I shall be saved. For thou art my praise. Behold, they say unto me, where is the word of Jehovah? Let it come now. As for me I have not hastened from being a shepherd after thee. Neither have I desired the woeful day. And this which came out of my lips was before thy face. Be not thou a terror unto me. Thou art my refuge in the day of evil (17:14-17).

The poet exhausts human similes to express the truth that God is intimate, real, a part of his own life's experience:

Thy words were found and I did eat them. And thy words were unto me a joy and the rejoicing of my heart (15:16).

Usually it is true that we find a relation between the quality of man's prayer life and the depth of his spiritual perception. Reading the poetry of Jeremiah one gains a picture of a man who is much in prayer, to whom prayer is natural, important, and real. Andrew Bonar, one of the saintliest of the modern preachers, left in his diary the record of a life of personal devotion which is the key to his spiritual power, a disclosure of the secret of his insights. These are some of the entries the reader finds:

By the grace of God and the strength of His Holy Spirit I desire to lay down the rule not to do anything with my hands until I have been on my knees. . . . . In prayer in the word for some time . . . . felt much drawn out to pray for that peculiar fragrance which believers have about them who are very much in

46

fellowship with God. With me every time of prayer or almost every time begins with a conflict. . . . . Today setting myself to prayer the Lord forthwith seemed to send a dew upon my soul.[1]

The reader of the Book of Jeremiah finds himself in the atmosphere of such a life of spiritual devotion. He feels that he has come upon a great soul at prayer. And the form and content of the prayers disclose the reality of the transactions between the soul and God. They suggest the likelihood of a stronger light falling upon the page for the man who thus knows God. Here, we feel, is the realization of that which a later, and a lesser, poet has put in his verse:

> Speak to Him thou, for He hears,
>   And Spirit with Spirit can meet.
> Closer is He than breathing,
>   And nearer than hands and feet.

THE LIFE OF SELF-COMMITMENT

There is one further testimony in the record of Jeremiah's life and utterances which sheds light upon the way truth came and possessed him. It is important for us to take it into account as we attempt to understand the processes of his illumination.

Jeremiah was, by the record of his life, predisposed to obey the will of God, to follow the light that he had. He began by yielding himself, not without remonstrance, to the call of God. Before the end of his days this became the passion of his life. No other prophet quite matches him in the complete commitment of his will to the will of God. Identity both with his message and with his people was his pronounced characteristic.

---

[1] Quoted in J. H. Jowett, *The Preacher: His Life and Work* (New York, Harper & Bros.).

His willingness to take the truth which came to him and obey it shines out in almost every critical choice in his career. He sighed for escape, "O that I had in the wilderness a lodge." But if some miracle had provided for him a lodge where he could get away from it all, he could not have occupied it long. Back he would be driven to take upon himself the burden of a life he just could not escape. He threw himself unremittingly into the life of his nation and shared the final agonies of those who went into captivity. He might have enjoyed the favor of the king, had he but spoken one word of hope and comfort. Yet with the experience of imprisonment behind him and the probability of more disgraceful punishment before him, he told the bitter truth. Where the truth led there he must go. More than any Old Testament personality he anticipated the word of Jesus, "The *truth* shall make you free." He gave the last full measure of devotion.

One of the facts of the spiritual life, proclaimed in Scripture and attested by experience, is that a pathway into the deeper knowledge of God is the will to obey God's will. A clearer light shines into the life of the man whose will is set to obey. Jesus declared this truth strikingly in this paradox: "If any man willeth to do His will he shall know the doctrine." As the eye is the medium of physical vision, so the soul is the medium of spiritual vision, and the more clear the medium, the more clear will be the vision. This is the import of His beatitude, "Blessed are the pure in heart, for they shall see God."

If it be true, as Frederick Robertson says, that "obedience is the organ of spiritual knowledge," we may expect that some individuals will enter more deeply than others into the apprehension of divine truth. Most men face the will of God, if they regard it at all, with certain selfish reservations in their hearts. They mark off areas in their lives and, like property owners, erect signs with the inscription, "Space within these lines not dedicated." Some high and rare souls march through life singing, and really meaning it: "I'll go where you want me to go, dear Lord." These are employing the true instrument of spiritual insight and, depending upon their capacity to receive, and the degree of their dedication, are led into the deeper, clearer knowledge of God.

There are laws and instruments operative in the realm of spiritual knowledge. Archbishop Söderblom pointed this out when he said, "In the kingdom of God no one can see so long as he remains merely a spectator. Those only who serve the will of God freely and sacrificially can see the will of God." [2] Dean Inge once suggested a truth with which all Christians may agree: "Have you ever thought," he said, "of the proportion of our waking life of some sixteen or seventeen hours which we devote to the ordinary affairs of this world as against five minutes of thinking about God and the soul, and of how inevitable it is that in consequence this world seems two hundred times more real than God and the environing world?" If, as St. Augustine said, there is a central Goodness who has created man for Himself, there must be possible transactions between the Creator and the child of His creation. Is it not likely that He who fulfills most completely the conditions, and who employs most fully the instruments of spiritual knowledge, will receive the fullest, clearest revelation? Given a man whose nature, both by inheritance and by cultivation, is especially sensitive to God and eternal values, whose heart has been stirred up by sincere and intense

---

[2] *The Nature of Revelation* (New York, Oxford Univ. Pr.), p. 168.

49

prayer and meditation, and whose will is prepared to go all the way, that man will inevitably become a channel through which the truth of God flows into human life.

Jeremiah was such a man, and the recognition of these elements in his capacity, his spiritual practice, and his volitional inclination prepares us for the last step in our answer to the question, "How did the word of the Lord come to Jeremiah?"

INTERPRETING LIFE

Recalling Jeremiah's insistence in his controversy with the professional prophets that he was clear-eyed and that he scorned their dreams and trances, we can readily see "how to the singer came the song." One difference that impresses us immediately between Jeremiah and men like Isaiah and Ezekiel is the absence of the vision, the ecstasy. He did not receive his call in the midst of a temple filled with light or surrounded by curious winged creatures. The revelations came to him not from cloven skies, or out of the midst of the thunders of the heavens. On the contrary the similes and parables which he describes as the starting point for his perception of divine truth are all objects or events of common, daily experience.

He sees a budding almond tree, first harbinger of reawakening life in the spring (1:11, 12), and because its name is like his word for "awake" it suggests to him that God is awake and watching over the life of man. And the conviction deepens until he must declare it, that God is living and presiding over the destinies of men and nations. He sees a caldron boiling, and its bubbles are toward the north (1:13-16). Brooding over the seething life of the nations, it becomes to him the symbol of the peril that will presently boil out of the north. It sets him upon a train of thought in which he sees

50

clearly the destructive nature of the sin which has infected the whole life of the nation. And he realizes that the rising power of the north, not the decadent empire of Egypt, will become the agent to visit destruction upon the heedless people.

He gives way to a mood of discouragement when his fellow townsmen turn against him and plot to destroy his life. And as he broods upon the meaning of it all he remembers a foot race and hears God asking him how he will contend against horsemen if he has been wearied running with footmen (12:5, 6). It becomes the call to save himself by losing himself in a greater task. He revolves in his mind the problem of a broken, failing nation and tries to reconcile it with the concept of a faithful God. And while the whole difficult problem brews in his mind he goes to the potter's house (18:1-3). There he sees a vessel marred under the hand of the potter and then by the potter broken on the wheel and refashioned into another vessel. And he knows that Judah must be finally broken. No half measures or reshaping will do. The nation must be completely broken. Then God can remake the true nation for His purposes.

Homely, everyday objects—a loin cloth, a basket of figs, a jar of water, paving stones—these are the only visions Jeremiah has. Every starting point of prophetic insight is just such an article as any man in Anathoth or Jerusalem might have seen any day. Yet through them came the word of the Lord to Jeremiah. It came not by magic, not apart from the faculties and capacities of the man himself. It was indeed the realization of the truth that "the word is very nigh thee, even in thy heart."

Whatever may be said about the *modus operandi* of the Holy Spirit as He "spake through holy men of old," one thing is clear about the inspiration of Jeremiah. He is a marked and positive example of God's working through the natural capacities of one individual to make known His will and way. This man who was tremendously aware of being laid hold upon by God was constantly employing the powers that God gives to men to arrive at the knowledge of His divine will.

The painting in the Sistine Chapel by Michelangelo includes a representation of Jeremiah that helps us to understand the processes of inspiration in the experience of this prophet. The artist does not represent Jeremiah as the traditional "weeping prophet," wringing his hands, and lamenting that the times are out of joint. He portrays him rather as a stalwart figure, creatively wrestling with the deep problems of his people. The canvas is comparable to Rodin's sculpture "The Thinker," or to John Drinkwater's dramatic representation of Abraham Lincoln's stern conflict as he comes through deep travail of soul to the point of affixing his signature to the Emancipation Proclamation. There sits the prophet, his head bowed, his eyes half closed as though to shut out every distracting scene. His hair is disheveled, suggesting a long period of self-forgetful concentration. His right hand covers his mouth and bearded chin. Every line of face and figure bespeaks the great strength of the man. The veins upon forehead and hand stand out, indicative of the inward struggle and the concentrated effort to see, not what man may desire, but what God wills. No flight of the imagination is necessary to perceive in this brooding personality a living picture of God and man working together to bring to light the will, and therefore, the word, of the Lord.

Possibly the most revealing example of this is that recorded in the forty-second chapter, when Johanan and the leaders of the remnant sought Jeremiah's counsel in a critical situation. The prophet promised them to lay the matter before God in prayer, "I will pray unto Jehovah . . . and whatsoever thing Jehovah shall answer you I will declare it unto you. I will keep nothing back from you" (42:4). He was not able to report to them the "word of the Lord" until ten days had passed. It is difficult to believe that in that ten-day interval Jeremiah was waiting for some "dream, a prophet ecstasy, a rending of the veil of clay." In the light of all that we know about his nature and behavior, we may believe that he was "watching and praying." He was making prayer to God and using his faculties—his clear vision, his statesmanlike perception, his powers of analysis to see the entire matter "steadily and see it whole." And after this period of brooding upon the problem, and of talking face to face with God, he was able to announce confidently, "The word of the Lord came to me."

In short, in the inspiration of Jeremiah we see two vital points. There is God, the Initiator, confronting an individual —confronting him through his capacities and faculties, confronting him because he is the kind of man that he is. And there is the individual, the respondent whose capacities, laid hold upon by God, are wholly yielded and applied to the God-imposed mission. And through this interaction, this co-operation between God and man, the will of God becomes the clear perception of the prophet, the glowing fire in his breast "which cannot be kept under." It is the word of God within the soul of man. And when he announces it to the nation he is speaking, as it were, "the oracles of God." His message, formed within him through this experience, and honestly proclaimed, becomes to mankind "the word of the Lord."

This is the People

"The Birth of a Nation" was the title of D. W. Griffith's contribution to patriotic arousement in the days preceding America's entrance into the first phase of world war. Designed to "stir up our minds by way of remembrance" this extravagant pageant unfolded episode after episode in the dawning, struggling, growing life of the state. It was a portrayal of beginnings. Looking through and beyond the drama one could envisage the quality of life, the spirit, and the conditions present upon this continent when "a new nation was brought forth."

"The Death of a Nation" could well be the title written over Baruch's record of the life and utterances of the prophet Jeremiah. For with a poetic imagery finer and sharper than the artistry of the modern dramatist, this ancient man of God unfolds the story of the last days of a nation. Grimly, undeviatingly, the tale proceeds from forecast, through all the stages of deterioration, to final tragic accomplishment. Jerusalem, long a battered pawn, expires in agony and a poet in a faraway land weeps out his lament, "By the waters of Babylon we sat down, yea, we wept, when we remembered Zion."

Jeremiah's record not only presents to us the story of these last days of Jerusalem, but his oracles disclose, for eyes that see, the conditions—moral, social, religious—that accompanied and surrounded this decline and, in his judgment, were the cause of it. They are a vivid reflection of the whole national situation. As the enactment of the Fugitive Slave Law smote with its impact the mind and soul of Ralph Waldo Emerson, it drew from his lips this searing speech: "There is infamy in the air. I have a new experience. I wake in the morning with a painful sensation which I carry about all day, and which, when traced home, is the odious remembrance of that ignominy which robs the landscape of beauty and takes the sunshine out of every hour." So Jeremiah, facing the multitude of infamies that marked the life of the state and the consequent disasters impending, was moved to pour out his emotions in a verse which bespeaks his anguish.

> My bowels, my bowels! O my pain!
>   O walls of my heart!
> My soul is tumult within;
>   I cannot keep still,
> For the trumpet's din in my ears,
>   The alarum of war.
> Crash upon crash it comes—
>   The ruin of all the land.
>
> —4:19-20; tr. by John Skinner

As each fresh infamy burst upon his amazed understanding and the hopelessness of the entire situation was brought home to him, this man who was a rare combination of poet, statesman, moral analyst, and historian celebrated the fact in verse or oracle which became a faithful picture of the national scene. Indeed, like Browning he could fittingly have given to selections of his verses the title, "How It Strikes a Contemporary."

55

It is the purpose of this chapter to look at this final and most instructive page of Hebrew history in the light of the poetry and oracles of one who was not only a spectator but a participant in the events that wrote the history. The last chapter of the book, written no doubt by another, contains this simple statement of historical fact: "This is the people that Nebuchadnezzar carried away into captivity." And then follows a numerical record of three deportations.

"This is the people." The writer of these words intended them merely to introduce the fact that some seven thousand people were translated from their beloved Jerusalem and set down by the waters of Babylon. But the reader of the Book of Jeremiah may well lift them from this association and place them as a preface to the prophet's report on the state of the nation. "This is the people that went into captivity." This is the *kind* of people that went into captivity, for whom captivity was an inevitable destiny. These are the conditions which according to one competent witness were present in the life of the nation as death approached, and which moved him to sigh for escape (how utterly modern his complaint!):

> O that I had in the desert
>   A wayfarer's lodge!
> For fain would I leave my people,
>   And go clean away.
> For adulterers are they all
>   A concourse of traitors.
> Falsehood and not good faith
>   Succeeds in the land;
> They hasten from evil to evil
>   And Me they know not, saith Jahwe.
>
> —9:2-4; tr. by John Skinner

Jeremiah's most scathing oracles present a clear picture of the religious situation of the day. His quarrel is not with a people who have lost their religion but with a religion which has lost its vital quality. He himself has experienced religion as heart-fellowship with the Eternal and the life of obedience that flows from this living union. And he is utterly shocked to discover that for his fellow-countrymen religion has become merely reliance upon an institution, the performance of certain ceremonies, and conformity to an external code without necessary reference to a living fellowship with a God whose worship in reality makes certain high ethical demands upon the worshiper.

It is to be recalled that Jeremiah's literature was produced in the atmosphere of a post-reformation period. The student must be mindful as he reads it of the great accomplishments of Josiah's reign initiated by the recovery of the Deuteronomic Code. His reform had abolished the shrines and outlawed the pagan practices of the fertility cults. It had established the temple of Jerusalem as the one center of religious worship and ceremony, and the Book of the Law as the one authority for civil as well as religious life. It had accomplished the reformer's dream and set up a purified religious system, buttressed by a sound code of laws. Superficially one would suppose that these ideal reforms should have satisfied the crusading spirit of a man like Jeremiah. Yet the significant fact disclosed by his oracles is their deep dissatisfaction with the life that proceeded from this very reformation. It was against the background of a sweeping religious and social reform that he delivered his temple sermon.

Thus saith Jehovah—Trust not in lying words, saying the temple, the temple, the temple of Jehovah are these. For if ye thoroughly amend your *ways* and your *doings*, if ye thoroughly execute justice between a man and his neighbor, if ye oppress not—then will I cause you to dwell in this place—behold ye trust in lying words that cannot profit. Will ye steal, murder, commit adultery and swear falsely, and burn incense to Baal and walk after other gods and come and stand before me in this house and say we are delivered, that ye may do all these abominations? Is this house that ye have called by my name become a den of robbers? (7:4-11).

Like One greater than he to come after him, Jeremiah thus stands in the very precincts of the temple and assails the religion which has lost its relevance to life and has become merely an institution under whose aegis the nation is presumed to be safe.

Stanley Jones in a sermon has described a fort at Jaipur which crowns a hill where once the life of the community centered. As years passed the city moved away and relocated itself on the plain some five miles distant. But on the hill, within the fort, the guard is changed daily, and the priests minister before the altar according to the ancient ritual. All the while these ceremonies are performed in the remote fort, the life of the community where people are born and grow up to love, hate, aspire, sorrow, rejoice, transact their business, and relate themselves to their fellow-men flows on five miles away, untouched and unconditioned by the traditional rites.

Jeremiah describes a religious system as remote and irrelevant as that. He heaps ridicule upon the idols and idol makers (10:1-10). Their very existence and trade betray the spiritual dullness of people whose God has so far receded from their lives that only an image can awaken the sense of deity. He thrusts at the people his question, "Wherefore is the land perished?" and flings back the answer, "Jehovah says, because they have forsaken my law which I have set before them and have not obeyed my voice, neither walked therein" (9:12, 13).

He takes his stand in the temple court itself after the reforms of Josiah have banished the shrines and idol worship, have recovered the law, and have made the one temple supreme, and yet he proclaims disaster for this sacred place if the spiritual worship of God as Reality be not recovered (chap. 26). In one of his most withering blasts he announces the hopelessness of the congregation which, like the faithless bride, has forsaken her husband.

> What has My darling to do in My house?
>   Vile are her doings.
> Can scraps of fat and sacred flesh
>   Turn calamity from thee?
> Then mightest thou rejoice
>   An olive tree, green, resplendent in beauty!—
> So wert thou called.
>   With noise of furious stormwind
> Its foliage blasted
>   Its branches destroyed.
>   —11:15-16; tr. by John Skinner

Jeremiah, in a word, sees a root condition from which, to his sensitive discernment, stem the evils that are imperiling the very existence of the nation. He sees a nation that has achieved the quality which a modern humanist hailed as the goal of an enlightened society—"religion without God."

LIFE WITHOUT INTEGRITY

A second characteristic of this people whom the prophet sees stumbling inevitably onward toward final captivity is made the theme of one of his most soaring verses:

Inquire among the nations:
    Who hath heard such a thing?
A thing appalling hath she done,—
    The Virgin of Israel.
Dissolves from Sirion's crest
    The spotless snow?
Or cease the mountain streams
    Their ice-cold flow?
But Me have my people forgotten
    They serve the unreal!
They have come to grief in their ways,
    The tracks of yore
Walking in paths uneven,
    A road unpaved.

—18:13-15; tr. by John Skinner

Jeremiah perceives that nature is held together by her integrity, by the constancy of her processes. This quality, simple integrity, has gone from the life of the nation. He laments that "falsehood and not good faith succeeds in the land." And no other failure stirs him more deeply.

If those critics are correct who place the poems of the fifth chapter at the beginning of his Jerusalem activity, we are given in them a glimpse of the amazement which sweeps over him as he begins to realize that fidelity has gone out of the life of these people among whom, because they live in the shadow of the restored temple, he had expected to find constancy. And when he discovers that lying, cheating, and dishonesty in speech and deed have become the rule of life of all whom he meets, he concludes that this must be because they are the uninstructed. So he turns to the nobles, "the great ones," and his dismay overwhelms him as he discovers that these privileged leaders have burst all bonds of decency and integrity. And with words that literally tumble over themselves he paints, for all ages to see, a picture of a life out of which, in high places and low, integrity has gone.

> Run through Jerusalem's streets,
>   And see for yourselves;
> And seek in her market places
>   If a man you can find,
> If one there be practicing right,
>   Or mindful of the truth.
> Nay when they say, As Jahwe lives,
>   They swear to a lie.
> Hast thou eyes then, O Jahwe, for fraud,
>   And not for good faith?
> Thou hast smitten them sore but they winced not;
>   They took no reproof;
> They have hardened their faces like flint,
>   Refusing to turn.
> I bethought me, these are the poor,
>   The ignorant folk
> Who know not the way of Jahwe,
>   The manner of their God,
> I will go to the men of high station,
>   With them will I talk;
> For they know the way of Jahwe,
>   The manner of their God,
> But they have quite broken the yoke
>   And burst the thongs.
>
> —5:1-5; tr. by John Skinner

The generation which has lived through two global disasters has little difficulty visualizing the quality of life that Jeremiah's poetry portrays. There are passages in which he speaks as a contemporary. The hearts of enlightened people were lifted and their hopes stimulated when, a generation ago, President Woodrow Wilson declared that, among other lofty principles which should end world strife and rule the

61

brave new world, dominant must be "open covenants, openly arrived at." To that principle the great nations of the world solemnly subscribed. And almost immediately began the era of secret covenants, secretly made. It culminated in the second outburst of world-wide conflagration in whose livid glare the universal reliance upon secret diplomacy was starkly revealed, and whose aftermath is disclosing a veritable maze of secret agreements that vitally affect human lives and national destiny.

Expediency—national, political, and ideological advantage —has appeared again and again to take precedence over integrity. Solemn covenants become scraps of paper. Scraps of paper become solemn covenants which may be made points of departure for that selfish national policy which suits the needs of the powerful and disposes of the destiny of peoples with no regard for lofty principles fervently proclaimed.

We who have seen nations shopping in the open market for allies, and political leaders casting about to determine upon which banner victory is destined to alight—that they may know with which contending power it were better to cast in their lot—can well understand the strictures of the prophets. More than a hundred years earlier than Jeremiah, Hosea looked at the indecision of the nation's leaders—another name for the lack of integrity and fidelity to principle—and indicted them for what he called their "silly dove" diplomacy, fluttering about from alliance to alliance, turning now to Egypt, now to Assyria, with some evidence of secret pacts with both powers (Hos. 7:11). Isaiah pleaded with the nation to realize that her security lay not in guessing which powerful state would emerge victorious and tying her future to a collaboration with that state, but in fidelity and steadfastness to God. "In returning and rest, shall ye be saved. In quietness and confidence shall be your strength" (Isa. 30:15).

Through the manifold changes of history the ancient policies of a decadent nation persisted. The voice of the men of vision was always lifted, a warning against the alliance as the way of security, and a call to return to the nation's true reliance upon God. The voice and manipulations of the opportunist leaders were always in the direction of power politics which ultimately prevailed and became the way of the nation. Fluttering like a "silly dove," the Northern Kingdom came at last into captivity in spite of protecting alliances hopefully made. The relentless march of history ultimately brought Assyria, the powerful conqueror and despoiler, to defeat, leaving two powers to contend for world domination, Egypt to the south and Babylon to the north.

Into this international scene Jeremiah was hurled. He strove heroically against the disintegration in Judah that followed the death of Josiah in the battle of Megiddo. Through the reigns of four kings, Shallum, Jehoiakim, Jehoiachin, and Zedekiah, he stubbornly resisted and eloquently denounced what seemed to him their fatal policy of seeking the alliance, of going to Egypt for security. He was aware of the deviousness, the undercover manipulations and secret pacts, that marked the diplomacy which brought final captivity to Israel. He was familiar with history's demonstration of the futility of the alliance as a weapon of security. He watched with dismay as the traditionalists in Jerusalem, led by the king, accustomed to seeing power residing in the older civilization to the south, urged that the future of the nation lay in remaining within Egypt's co-prosperity sphere. Apparently no one remembered the incisive sarcasm of Hosea, the steady wisdom of Isaiah, or the fatal outcome of Israel's policy of collaboration. Of this Jeremiah sought in vain to remind the nation.

Why do you change your way? You shall be put to the blush through Egypt also as you were through Assyria (2:36).

Facing this situation with its manifest departure from that constancy which he saw so clearly as the cohesive, salutary force in life, he lifted his voice in picturesque and pungent warning against the way of diplomacy.

> Yea the sons of Memphis and Daphnai
> > Shall shave thee bald.
> Is not this the result of departing
> > From Jahwe thy God?
> And now, why goest thou to Egypt
> > Nile water to drink?
> And why dost thou go to Assyria
> > To drink of the stream?
> Let thine own misfortune reprove thee!
>
> —2:16-19; tr. by John Skinner

Such deviousness, to this man of God, could only spell the "way of death."

There are other pictures. One more only can be considered here. It becomes particularly vivid in the light of the shallow insincere repentances and repeated lapses which are so shameful a part of our own recent wartime experience. Among Jeremiah's last conflicts in Jerusalem was one which disclosed the utter loss of integrity and called forth from him his most biting word of scorn, and prophecy of doom. When the siege of Jerusalem by the Chaldeans was at its height the slave owners remembered their covenant which forbade the imposition of perpetual slavery upon their fellow Hebrews.

And as disaster seemed imminent and they and the slaves, too, were likely to be made captive at any rate, they set the slaves free. "When the devil was sick! . . ." Just after this liberation was consummated the approach of an Egyptian army caused the Chaldeans to lift the siege. Whereupon the Israelites, the pressure now removed, promptly recaptured their slaves. Shocked and dismayed by this final evidence of treachery, Jeremiah gave voice to one of his most powerful oracles.

Thus saith Jehovah: Ye have not hearkened unto me to proclaim liberty every man to his brother and every man to his neighbor; behold I proclaim unto you a liberty, saith Jehovah, to the sword, to the pestilence, to the famine, and I will make you to be tossed to and fro among the nations of the earth.—The princes of Judah, and the princes of Jerusalem, the eunuchs and the priests—I will give them into the hands of their enemies, and into the hands of them that seek their life, and their dead bodies shall be for food to the birds of the heavens and to the beasts of the earth. And Zedekiah king of Judah and his princes will I give into the hand of them that seek their life, and into the hand of the king of Babylon's army that are gone away from you. Behold I will command, saith Jehovah, and cause them to return to this city to fight against it, and take it and burn it with fire; and I will make the cities of Judah a desolation without inhabitant (34: 17-22).

Plainly in the mind of Jeremiah there is the settled conviction that an incurable disease is at work in the life of the nation. "Falsehood and not good faith succeeds in the land." Slowly, and we may believe reluctantly, he comes to the position that external measures, social reform, even religious rehabilitation cannot halt the creeping paralysis, and only death awaits the people infected by this virus. He sees that life without integrity is destined to move on to complete destruction, and he voices his lament:

> Ah thou deceitful city!
> All extortion within!
> As a cistern keeps cool its waters,
> So she her evils.
> Rapine and outrage are heard in her;
> Before Me are evermore sickness and wounds.

> —6:6, 7; tr. by John Skinner

The Flesh Without Control

The earlier prophets had all spoken solemn warnings against an evil which throughout human history has been the accompaniment of a ripening civilization, that is, abandonment to the sensual. The usual cycle was completing its course in the life of the Hebrew nation. That cycle may be traced through its successive stages: first, struggle, rise, and mastery, accompanied by certain disciplines and moral restraints; then affluence, power, and exploitation, marked by wide social divergencies and an increase of sophisticated living and sensual indulgence; and finally decline and deterioration, hastened by an abandonment to the sensual.

Against these manifestations in the life of both the Northern and Southern Kingdoms the prophets of the spirit had all contended. Isaiah, Amos, and Hosea especially have left striking pictures of the state of a society overripe. Their period has been described with a suggestive imagery as "Israel's Indian Summer."

Jeremiah finds Judah in her last days no exception to this pattern. He sees this quality working itself out in its usual manifestations. Heartless greed and crafty oppression are the marks of the privileged classes.

Yea, rogues are found in my people
Who set snares to do for men.
As a cage is full of birds
So their houses of unjust gain,
Hence they are grown great and rich,
They are fat and stout.
They espouse not the cause of the orphan,
Nor defend the right of the widow.

—5:26-28; tr. by John Skinner

A sharp picture of the unbridled exercise of power for selfish material ends and of the widening chasm between the privileged and the underprivileged is presented by the prophet's stern denunciation of King Jehoiakim. The monarch had employed his power to build a sumptuous and impressive palace, using what amounted virtually to slave labor. This callousness moved Jeremiah to one of his most courageous and impassioned speeches, gleaming with sarcastic thrusts.

Woe to him that builds his home with injustice
    His storeys with wrong!
Who makes his fellow-men serve for nought,
    And keeps back his wage.
Who says I will build me a spacious house,
    With roomy chambers;
Well lighted with windows, paneled with cedar,
    And bright with red paint!
Is it thus thou wouldst play the King—
    By outvieing in cedar?
Did not thy father eat and drink
    And do himself well?
Yet he practiced justice and right,
    Judged the cause of the needy and poor:
Was not this to know Me in truth?
        saith Jahwe.
    But thou hast nor eyes nor thought

67

For aught save thy gain:
   For the innocent blood thou canst shed,
The murder thou canst do.

—22:13-17; tr. by John Skinner

The ascendency of the sensual, Jeremiah sees too, working itself out in crass indulgence and licentious living. Excesses of the flesh smite him on every hand. His poetry gives us a vivid picture of the flesh without control. After he has been shocked by the lack of integrity, which he attributes at first only to the ignorant and underprivileged, he turns to "the great ones," expecting to find among them the way of the Lord. And here he discovers that which brings deepest dismay to his soul. These people who have prospered—sleek, well-fed, privileged people—have followed the course to which a prosperous estate has so often lured, the course of selfish, sensual indulgence. And an age which has become surfeited by the tale of lewdness, infidelity, crass indulgence thrust upon it in its contemporary literature, art, and drama, as well as in the personalities and philosophies of many of its public figures, is prepared to understand Jeremiah's graphic picture of his own day:

When I had fed them to the full they committed adultery; and assembled themselves in troops at the harlots' houses. They were as fed horses roaming at large; every one neighed after his neighbor's wife. Shall I not visit for these things, and be avenged upon such a nation as this? (5:7-9).

The greedy indulgence of every lower passion, from which no class is exempt, has furthermore accomplished in its practitioners a perversion of judgment, a loss of moral sense. False practice has bred false standards.

For even from the least of them unto the greatest, every one is given unto covetousness, and from the prophet to the priest every one dealeth falsely. They have healed also the hurt of my people slightly, saying, Peace, peace, when there is no peace. Were they ashamed when they committed abominations? Nay they were not ashamed, *neither could they blush* (6:13-15).

There is one deft touch in these complaints of Jeremiah which tells a significant story. After he has described the manner in which the powerful and the crafty employ their opportunity for selfish gain, he adds this: "The prophets prophesy falsely: and the priests bear rule by their means; and *my people love to have it so;* and what will ye do in the end thereof?" (5:31).

There is hope for a people, a nation, a civilization in which evil leaders and evil practices have gained a footing if the people do not become "corrupt and contented." Evil measures, evil practices, evil leaders there may be, but Jeremiah abandons hope when "the people love to have it so."

RELIANCES WITHOUT THE SOUL

As the life and vigor of Judah slowly ebb and she moves toward her inevitable captivity, Jeremiah sees yet another characteristic contributing to her destiny. In the days of the nation's robust, free life her leaders were not men who did no sin, but men who were capable of seeing sin and turning the eyes of their people toward the right. Her men of the spirit spoke to the conscience of the people and there was a response. Sometime in their history one of their sages said, "Where there is no vision the people perish." Jeremiah is living in a day when this truth is finding its bitter fulfillment. The nation has lost her spiritual vision and her reliances are all the things which can be seen and measured. In short, she

69

has reached that stage where the idolatry of human powers and achievement has fully ripened.

The priests said not, where is Jehovah? and they that handle the law knew me not. The rulers also transgressed against me, and the prophets prophesied by Baal and walked after things that do not profit (2:8).

This self-idolatry, which has become so pronounced a feature of the nation's life, is seen in its relation to the national destiny in a verse whose insight is particularly keen.

> Thus saith the Lord,
> Boast not the wise in his wisdom,
> Boast not the strong in his strength,
> Boast not the rich in his riches,
> But he that would boast in this let him boast,
> Insight and knowledge of Me
> That I am the Lord who worketh truth.
>
> —9:23, 24; tr. by George Adam Smith

The crowning picture of all, revealing the self-idolatry of the nation, is the reading of the scroll to King Jehoiakim. Jeremiah was moved to gather his various messages and oracles, which to him were so definitely the word of the Lord to the nation, and commit them to parchment. Baruch was his scribe, and after painstaking effort the labor was completed. The scroll was read first to the people, then later to the king in the presence of the noblemen of his court. As the reading progressed Jehoiakim—haughty, contemptuous ruler, seated by a fire—took his knife and deliberately cut the parchment into strips and tossed them into the fire. Not even the incisive messages of a man like Jeremiah could touch his spirit and awaken in him the vision of a higher King "beneath whose hand he held dominion over palm and pine."

70

There is in Tennyson's "Holy Grail" a subtle presentation of a profound truth when the poet describes the tower Merlin built for Arthur. He pictures in its four zones of sculpture the steady rise of man: mastered first by the beasts, then master of the beasts, rising then as a warrior to master his own kind, and finally aspiring to soar in the heavens, growing wings. He then crowns the mighty hall with the statue of Arthur in the mold of a king, "so high, so bright against the sky that the peasants in the distant fields can look up and see it, and say 'we still have a King.'" No matter how high life rises in its mastery, the poet means to say, it is lost if it gets beyond the vision of the King, high and lifted up.

The scene in the hall of Jehoiakim leaves with us a picture of men whose vision of the higher reliance has wholly perished.

Now the king was sitting in the winter house in the ninth month; and there was a fire in the brazier burning before him. And it came to pass when Jehudi had read three or four leaves that the king cut it with his penknife and cast it into the fire that was in the brazier until all the roll was consumed. . . . . And they were not afraid, nor rent their garments neither the king nor any of his servants who heard these words (36:22-24).

Jehoiakim, arrogant, self-sufficient monarch, devoid of spiritual vision, warming himself with the shreds of the document that might have brought living warmth to the nation, is the epitome of all the "strong who boast in their strength." History has witnessed many stern ironies. None, not even the death of Hitler's Reich, exceeds that of the contrast between this scene and those surrounding the destruction of Jerusalem by the Chaldeans, "that bitter and hasty nation."

71

Then the king of Babylon slew the sons of Zedekiah before his eyes: also the king of Babylon slew all the nobles of Judah. Moreover he put out Zedekiah's eyes and bound him in fetters to carry him to Babylon. And the Chaldeans burned the king's house and the houses of the people with fire and brake down the walls of Jerusalem (39:6-8).

The fire that burned in the brazier had at last burned itself out.

This, then, is the people that went into captivity. Jeremiah in his report on the state of the nation thus takes his place in the company of those analysts, ancient and modern, who discern a predictable pattern in the course of declining nations and civilizations. The nation, to his penetrating eyes, was carrying within itself the seeds of its own death. Oswald Spengler, among modern students of history, sees a similar condition in all the civilizations that he subjects to his careful scrutiny. He traces each great culture through its cycle of spring, summer, fall, and winter and discovers identical qualities of life present in each as the cycle completes itself. Arnold Toynbee, studying twenty-one civilizations, finds in twenty of them (the twenty-first is not completed) as they rise, come to their zenith, and die, a common denominator. Jeremiah's vision, although sweeping a less expansive horizon, rests upon a similar scene.

A visitor to Edinburgh Castle once remarked upon the apparent impregnability of that ancient citadel in the day for which it was originally designed and constructed. He asked a guide how it was ever possible for an enemy, with only the primitive weapons of that early day, to capture the fort. After a moment's thought the guide replied: "No enemy ever really captured it. When it fell it was because of some failure within the walls, the lack of food, or water, or more frequently the treachery of some of the defenders." Jeremiah's literature discloses unmistakably that this was his interpretation of history and of the impending doom. He saw the punishment for moral and spiritual failure not in some arbitrary decree of a vast lawgiver, nor in some celestial thunderbolt hurled by an outraged deity, but in the inevitable death inherent in the failure itself. He saw the Babylonian king and his army as the external instruments, the tools by which the defeat was fashioned. But the real disaster was proceeding from within the life of the nation. If the malady within could not be healed, and he was finally convinced that it could not —"The sin of Judah is written with a pen of iron and with a point of diamond; it is graven upon your heart" (17:1)— there could be no turning aside of the doom to which the nation was inevitably moving. Whatever the external instrument of the denouement, the actual compulsion was to be found within Judah—"Be thy scourge thine own sin"— and as the nation stumbled on to irretrievable disaster, Jeremiah composed his verse in which posterity could read for itself his interpretation of the destiny.

> Hear and give ear and be not proud:
>> For Jahwe hath spoken.
> Give Jahwe, your God, the glory,
>> Ere it grow dark;
> Before your feet stumble
>> On darkening mountains
> And you wait for light but darkness is there,
>> And he turns it to gloom.
> In secret my soul shall weep
>> Because of your pride;
> And my eye run down with tears,
>> For Jahwe's flock is led captive.
>
> —13:15-17; tr. by John Skinner

The God of Jeremiah

"Men have come to believe that there is nothing in God to fear and nothing in sin to worry about." In thus accounting for a moral letdown in the life of his day, William Gladstone testified to the relation between the theology of men and their behavior. If he had been essaying a summary of the prophet Jeremiah's appraisal of the religious and moral situation of his time he could scarcely have hoped for better success. For Jeremiah perceived very clearly that low and false views of God translate themselves into low standards and crooked practices in the life of man. And all that he said and wrote bears the unmistakable stamp of this perception. Contemplating the faithless, sensual, greedy life of his people, he traced it to the manifest loss of awareness of the living God. And he set forth this sequence in a body of literature in whose content a modern writer like Edna St. Vincent Millay might well have found her inspiration as she wrote in *Conversation at Midnight*, "Man has never been the same since God died."

It is in this insight that the student of Jeremiah's writings finds the prophet's most valuable contribution to his religion's thought of God. Other spokesmen of God contribute other insights. One looks in vain in the writings of Jeremiah for that aura of mystery, that inexpressible transcendence which

74

characterizes many of Scripture's exalted passages. God does not speak to Jeremiah from a "stormy wind cloud, with a fire infolding itself and a brightness round about it, as it were glowing metal." The language and the symbols that would conceivably become a part of the ritual of adoration are not to be derived from this prophet. Nor is Jeremiah a didactic theologian. One does not discern in him a "line upon line, precept upon precept" teaching concerning the nature of God. The theistic arguments are no part of his method. He is rather like the sturdy Norwegian pastor of Trygve Gulbranssen's *Wind From the Mountains*. "Pastor Ramer did not mount the pulpit to philosophize an excuse for God being possibly—and unfortunately—in existence. He . . . so believed in God that the whole Church lived." So the God of Jeremiah is to be discerned in the prophet's great assumptions in prayer, in his calls to individual and national strength of character, and in his moral indignation at the failures of his people, whose failures he traces to their loss of God. And the God thus disclosed becomes very clear and real upon all his pages.

Marc Connelly's drama, *Green Pastures*, opens with a prologue in which a Negro child in a Sunday-school class asks his teacher the question: "What is God like?" The teacher answers the child's question by saying "Well, as nearly as I can tell He must be like the Rev. DuBois," and then the drama unfolds in a series of episodes depicting the unlettered Negro's idea of God—the very real, personal God whom the old parson knew and preached. The child's question is the perennial question of mankind, asked with varying degrees of intellectual apprehension, but always with the stubborn demand for certitude. "Today," says A. N. Whitehead in *Religion in the Making*, "there is but one religious dogma in debate: What do you mean by God? And in this respect today is like all the yesterdays. This is the fundamental religious dogma."[1]

Many answers, some crude, some simple, some profound and erudite, have been given to this question. One New Testament writer has said "God who in former times hath spoken through the prophets, hath in these latter days spoken through His Son, Christ Jesus." Jeremiah manifestly belongs to the goodly fellowship of the prophets through whom God spoke in the former times. The full "light of the knowledge of the glory of God in the face of Christ Jesus" had not yet been revealed. But the literature of this man of the former days is most instructive for those who would seek an answer to the age-old, world-wide question, "What is God like?" Its instruction is to be found by singling out certain great passages and episodes, and marking the basic assumptions, the undergirding convictions, the outflashings of insight and revelation there. And over these may be inscribed for the prophet the title: "My Idea of God."

ONE GOD, THE FATHER ALMIGHTY

At the very basis of Jeremiah's idea of God stands a quality not at all peculiar to his perception, but set forth with a peculiar incisiveness. The God whom Jeremiah knew existed as the absolute sovereign of all creation. "Thou shalt have no other gods before me" was for him not just a decree graven upon a tablet of stone. It was a tremendous, life-conditioning fact, significant because it was graven first of all upon the constitution of life itself. There are ways and ways of saying "I believe in God the Father Almighty, Maker of heaven and earth." Confessionally minded people

---

[1] The Macmillan Co., New York, p. 67 f.

76

may recite it complacently in the midst of comfortable surroundings and traditional circumstances with no awareness of an implication for the whole life of the worshiper. They frequently do. On the other hand, a man may say this word as the expression of a profound fact before which every item of his life's choices, attitudes, and behavior bows down. Jeremiah's concept of God was of this order. To him the sovereignty of God was never merely a part of a system of theology. It was a controlling reality of life. There was one fundamental conviction which he could never compromise, one passion which he expressed with characteristic intolerance. Others could think and speak of the deities men devise and worship as false gods. To Jeremiah they were "no gods." His monotheism went all the way. It was declared in his repeated phrase *Lo Elohim*. "Hath a nation changed its gods, which are yet no gods?" (2:11). "Thy children have forsaken me and sworn by them that are no gods" (5:7). "Shall a man make unto himself gods that are no gods?" (16:20). Jeremiah unites himself in a living fellowship across the centuries with those who affirm from the heart, "I believe in *one* God, the Father Almighty."

His conception of the divine sovereignty is to be seen in the amazement with which he contemplates his people's transgression. The fifth chapter of his book contains one of the most vivid analyses and most striking arraignments of sin, individual and social, to be found in any literature. But the prophet is not content with the mere uncovering and denunciation of sin. Significantly enough he crowns his whole arraignment with a word whose import may not be missed. The enormity of this sin, to his discerning spirit, is not the wrong done to the individual, or even to the nation, but the rebellion against God which is at the root of it. It is the self-assertiveness of man against the sovereignty of God. "There is nothing in God to fear." This is the profound import of the question which the prophet flings as the climax of his indictment:

Fear ye not me? saith Jehovah; will ye not tremble at my presence, who have placed the sands for the bound of the sea, by a perpetual decree that it cannot pass it? And though the waves thereof toss themselves yet can they not prevail; though they war, yet can they not pass over it (5:22).

This perception of the absolute sovereignty of God is the very basis of most of Jeremiah's declarations of duty and definitions of righteousness. It gives confidence to his speech. It creates wrath against evildoers. They are fighting God. It is the theme of his prayer—32:16-25—which will receive later consideration. It undergirds many of his most moving speeches. God is the Creator "who giveth the sun for a light by day and the ordinances of the moon and of the stars for a light by night, who stirreth up the sea so that the waves thereof roar. Jehovah of hosts is his name" (31:35). Jeremiah thus joins the goodly company of those poets, philosophers, and seers who are moved by their contemplation of creation's processes to reverence for the Creator. Immanuel Kant was filled with awe by two things: the vast order of the starry universe without, and the moral law within. Centuries before, a herdsman of Tekoa rebuked the vaunting arrogance of unrighteous men by pointing to them the rule of the sovereign God: "Ye who turn justice to wormwood and cast down righteousness to the earth, seek him that maketh the Pleiades and Orion and turneth the shadow of death into morning, and maketh the day dark with night, that calleth forth the waters of the sea and poureth them out on the earth

(Jehovah is His name)" (Amos 5:7-9). A poet of the Hebrew people sang in immortal verse the same great truth—"when I consider thy heavens, the work of thy hands, the moon and the stars which thou hast ordained; what is man, that thou art mindful of him, or the son of man, that thou visitest him?" (Ps. 8:3, 4). Like these great souls, Jeremiah looks at the laws and processes of nature with eyes that are open to behold the Power who contrived them, and in his own way reverently continues his affirmation of faith, "I believe in one God, the Father Almighty, Maker of all things visible and invisible."

The idea of a sovereign God is even more clearly discerned in the prophet's presentation of God as the Fashioner of the lives and destinies of men. Possibly the clearest delineation of this is in the parable of the potter's vessel recorded in the eighteenth chapter. A faithful interpretation of this incident goes far beyond the common reference of it to the experiences of individual life—"Thou art the potter, we are the clay"—and emphasizes Jeremiah's understanding of the absolute sovereignty of God.

Here is no mere facile seizure and use of an artificer's practice to illumine the processes of God in dealing with individuals. Here is rather a flash of insight into the power and the right of God to shape, to crush, to refashion the destinies of individuals and nations, a far more radical and inclusive thing.

In the midst of his perplexity as he watched the deterioration of the national situation and wrestled with the doubts induced by it, Jeremiah made his way to the house of a potter. The question which was thrusting itself into his consciousness was, "How can we believe that God's purpose for the chosen people holds as we see the inevitable approach of their doom?" "Where is now thy God?" Then he saw the potter fashioning a vessel, and the vessel became marred under his hand. The potter did not attempt to reshape the marred vessel. He deliberately and irrevocably broke it upon the wheel and reshaped it into another vessel. Light began to dawn upon the perplexed prophet. If sometimes the potter must crush and destroy his creation so that his ultimate purpose may be accomplished through a complete refashioning, so indeed may God break and crush this vessel of His making, that the true end of His creation may ultimately be realized. This nation—"wholly intractable stuff"—can no longer fulfill its destiny as it now exists. Mere readjustments, smoothing of rough surfaces, altering of exterior details, a correction here, a revision there, will no longer avail. The vessel itself must be broken. The nation must be crushed, all its institutions completely destroyed and a new nation formed under the hand and according to the design of God. *And God has the power and the right to do this* as much as the potter who employs his skill and art to refashion the marred vessel.

From this experience Jeremiah went out to preach and counsel with an unshakable certainty a message that to his compatriots seemed traitorous. He declared that Judah's only hope lay in surrendering to the enemy. In the headlines of the daily newspaper his counsel would be that of defeatism and could be stigmatized as treachery. In the tomes of history, it was farseeing statesmanship. It rested upon his profound recognition of that which Abraham Lincoln once expressed, "This nation under God."

Not only did Jeremiah know God as the sovereign of His chosen people. He recognized Him as Lord of lords and King of kings. Today Judah must go down to defeat in the crushing experience. Babylon will rise to the place of power and domination, as conqueror and ruler of the nations. But tomorrow Babylon, transgressing the inherent laws of the Sovereign God, will also go the way of the fallen nations. The conqueror shall be conquered.

Jeremiah thus resolves quite simply the obvious question that is raised by his prediction, "How can God use as His instruments such a cruel, wicked nation as the Babylonians?" They are more wicked than the Hebrews whom they devour. Habakkuk's whole prophecy, it will be remembered, revolved about this very problem. He first flung at God the skeptic's question, "How long shall I cry and thou wilt not hear?" When God showed him that he was preparing the Chaldeans to rebuke and punish the sinful nation, his perplexity was only increased. "O Jehovah, thou hast ordained him for judgment . . . thou that art of purer eyes than to behold iniquity, wherefore lookest thou upon them that deal treacherously?" (Hab. 1:12, 13). His prophecy unravels that problem thread by thread.

But Jeremiah, facing exactly the same perplexity, settles it for himself with utter directness and consistency. The Chaldeans are subject to the same immutable law. They too shall be destroyed. Nebuchadnezzar will rule only "until the time of his own land come." In his advice to the exiles (chap. 29), the prophet speaks of restoration within seventy years. By that time the cycle of the conqueror's power will have run its course. There is no escape from the law. It operates toward all alike. Jeremiah would say, "Except ye repent ye shall *all* likewise perish." He foresees doom as the inevitable result of any favored nation's self-assertiveness against that divine, eternal rule at the heart of the universe.

I have made the earth, the men, and the beasts that are upon the face of the earth, by my great power, and by my outstretched arm, and I give it *unto whomsoever it seemeth right to me*. And now I have given all these lands into the hands of Nebuchadnezzar . . . and all nations shall serve him *until the time of his own land come:* and then many nations and great kings shall make him their bondman (27:5-7).

The insight of this speech was abundantly vindicated by history. Nebuchadnezzar, looking about him at the proud achievements and the might of his empire, exclaimed: "Is not this mighty Babylon which I have builded?" And the next generation saw the handwriting on the wall: "Thou art weighed in the balances and found wanting, and thy kingdom is divided and given to the Medes and Persians." Jeremiah perceived so acutely that above all the accomplishments and power and pretensions of men is God whose sovereignty men may refuse to acknowledge, but who throughout history has always had the last word. The "Recessional" by which the prophet vainly sought to call the nation's leaders and people back to God has been repeated by other voices in other measures. A poet of Israel sang it thus: "Why do the heathen rage and the people imagine a vain thing? The kings of the earth set themselves against the Lord and against his anointed, saying, 'Come, let us break their bonds asunder, let us cast their cords from us.' He that sitteth in the heavens shall laugh" (Ps. 2:1-4).

A modern poet has sung the same theme:

> The tumult and the shouting dies;
>   The captains and the kings depart:
> Still stands Thine ancient sacrifice,
>   An humble and a contrite heart.
>
> If drunk with sight of power we loose
>   Wild tongues that have not Thee in awe,

Such boastings as the Gentiles use,
  Or lesser breeds without the Law—
Lord God of Hosts, be with us yet,
Lest we forget—lest we forget!
            From "Recessional," RUDYARD KIPLING.

"And when they forgot God," the kingdom has always been divided and given to some Medes and Persians. He that sitteth in the heavens has laughed.

THE LIVING GOD

A second quality of the God whose presence pervades Jeremiah's literature is set forth with equal vividness. The God of Jeremiah was living and active. That truth about God which was struggling for expression in the Hebrews' definition "I am" was a pronounced feature of the picture that was upon the screen of the prophet's mind when he spoke of God. It is seen most clearly as it stands contrasted against the ideas of God currently prevalent. To the legalist of Jeremiah's day God was a faraway deity to be found and worshiped through certain prescribed ceremonies, in certain appointed places, and through conformity to a definite code. To the spiritually dull who lapsed into frequent and varied idolatries God could be visualized only through an image, the dead creation of men's hands, dependent upon its creators for locomotion. To the speculative mind God was a theorem to be demonstrated, a problem of theological debate, an entity to be defined and described.

Against all these pictures that came before the minds of men as the question "What do you mean by God?" was asked there stands the God of Jeremiah, living and active. The oft-repeated phrase, "Jehovah that doeth it" (33:2), epitomizes the prophet's thought in this respect. He was not able to think of his God as far away in the heavens, waiting for the incense of a worshiper's sacrifice to reach Him. He could not conceive of Him in the terms of an image that the worshiper must move from place to place. Most pointedly, he could not pray to a speculative formula. The God of Jeremiah was the living God, "Jehovah that doeth it."

The prophet himself tells how the awareness of this quality became an imperative factor in his call. Back of the call, which he records faithfully, there must have been some wrestlings of the spirit, of which there is no record. Contemplating the course his nation was pursuing and the ruin it portended, he no doubt asked the question that perplexed minds have ever lifted: "Is God dead?" His question was resolved for him, and his own course charted by the conviction that God was living and active. As Jeremiah looked back over the processes which impelled him to his ministry he could never forget the vision of the almond tree. He gave the experience its significant place in his narrative because in it God opened his eyes to a transforming truth. He made Jeremiah aware that the Creator had not abandoned His world, but that He was alive, presiding over all its movements, operative in all its life. And as the prophet told the story of the vision certain words must have been underscored in his own mind. "The word of Jehovah came to me saying, what seest thou? And I said, I see an almond tree. Then said Jehovah, thou hast well seen: for *I watch over my word to perform it*" (1:11, 12). The truth which dawned upon his consciousness in that vision grew in its meaning until he saw it in all its implications for his own life and the life of the nation, and in its international applications as well. It became a determining force in his judgments and in all his messages.

84

God is not a silent spectator of the affairs of life. He is not a "primary force" who created the universe, set it running, and retired into the vast unknown while nature played out its role. Jeremiah knew God as reality, living, contending in the arena of human affairs. "The priests said not, where is Jehovah? And they that handle the law knew me not; the rulers also transgressed against me, and the prophets prophesied by Baal and walked after things that do not profit. Wherefore I will yet contend with you, saith Jehovah, and with your children's children will I contend" (2:8, 9).

The God of Jeremiah was providence. "O generation, seek ye the word of Jehovah. Have I been a wilderness unto Israel? or a land of thick darkness?" (2:31). The prophet summons the most picturesque, living terms to call his people to an awareness of a living God, a God who moves and acts in the area of human experience.

One of the finest bits of satire ever written has this thought of God as its abiding message. With biting sarcasm the prophet describes the making of the idol by people whose spiritual sense has become so dull that they can conjure up the idea of God only through the visible image. Scornfully he jibes at the idol makers for the helplessness of their god. Sadly he contemplates the reduction of the idea of God to the stature of this inanimate device.

For the customs of the people are vanity: for one cutteth a tree out of the forest, the work of the hands of the workman with the axe. They deck it with silver and gold; they fasten it with nails and with hammers that it move not. They are like a palm tree, of turned work, and speak not: they must needs be borne because they cannot go. Be not afraid of them; for they cannot do evil, neither is it in them to do good. . . . There is silver beaten into plates, which is brought from Tarshish, and gold from Uphaz, the work of the artificer and of the hands of the goldsmith; blue and purple for their clothing: they are all the work of skillful men. But Jehovah is the true God. He is the living God and an everlasting King (10:3-10).

The commandment which is the foundation of the Decalogue had for centuries thundered its message to the people: "Thou shalt not make unto thee any graven image." The worshipers of God must keep alive spirituality in worship. The abiding reason for this demand was also declared in the same commandment, "I am the Lord thy God *which brought thee out of the land of Egypt, out of the house of bondage.*" The spiritual worship of God depended upon the recognition of that God as providence, living activity. This the nation forgot, and so the people fashioned their idols. But Jeremiah never forgot it. And against a spiritual deadness that resorted to idols and idol making he proclaimed the eternity and final lordship of the living God.

The gods that have not made the heavens and the earth, these shall perish from the earth and from under the heavens. . . . Every goldsmith is put to shame by his graven image, for his molten image is falsehood and there is no breath in them. They are a vanity, a work of delusion: in the time of their visitation they shall perish. The portion of Jacob is not like these, and Israel is the tribe of his inheritance. Jehovah of hosts is his name (10:11-16).

"RIGHTEOUS ART THOU"

The poetry and oracles of Jeremiah indicate that he knew God not only as supreme, God of gods, and as living; but more deeply, he knew Him as a holy and righteous God. This is the most pronounced feature of his conception of God and is at once the key to his life of prophetic activity. In this again he is not unique among the prophets. Isaiah's presentation of the demands of a righteous God is reflected in all the preaching of Jeremiah. He preached no new theme in declaring the righteousness of God. But he gave forceful emphasis to a fundamental truth in a day when it had all but become lost. And he did it in a manner and with an application that have made it unforgettable.

When man's god becomes the projection of his own thought, even his best thought, not only is his god unworthy; his own life, individual and social, is in peril. Distorted ideas of God mean a distorted life of man. To Jeremiah the chief evil of the sin of his people was that it was evidence of their loss of God. "Man has never been the same since God died." The source of the good life of man was for him the holiness of God. He did not say it, but his whole prophetic message proclaimed in the name of God, "Be ye holy even as I am holy." The reason for a righteous life on earth was the essential righteousness which was at the source and center of all things. The condemnation of the falseness of men was the *integrity* of *God*.

This truth, both in its divine fact and its human implication, is pointedly declared in the first record of the temple sermon.

Thus saith Jehovah of hosts, amend your *ways* and *your doings*, and I will cause you to dwell in this place. Say not the temple of Jehovah, the temple of Jehovah, the temple of Jehovah, are these. For if ye thoroughly amend your ways and your doings, if ye execute righteousness . . . if ye oppress not, if ye shed not innocent blood, and walk not after other gods . . . I will cause you to dwell in this place, in the land that I gave to your fathers (7:3-7).

To the discerning spirit of Jeremiah there is an inseparable relation between the holiness of God and the responsibility

87

for righteous living that rests upon the worshipers of this God. In the ninth chapter, after describing the deceit and treachery and evil that are rampant, the prophet declares the oracle of God in one of the most revealing words in his book: "Behold I will melt them and try them, for *how else should I do* because of the daughter of my people?" (9:7). The very character of God requires the trial and melting. There is nothing else that He *can* do without denying the holiness which is the essence of His Being. Jeremiah's insight is especially keen when he represents the punishment of sin as not at all the arbitrary decree of an offended Deity, but the operation of an inherent principle. "Thine own wickedness shall correct thee, and thy backsliding shall reprove thee: know therefore and see that it is an evil thing and a bitter that thou hast forsaken Jehovah thy God, and my fear is not in thee" (2:19). Thus, centuries before St. Paul, Jeremiah announces one half of the Apostle's "Little Gospel"—"the wages of sin is death." It is so not because the pronouncement of an overlord has made it so, but because the essential holiness of God requires that it be so.

Occasionally the prophet's speech soars to great heights as he gives full, poetic voice to his conception of God. Always the overtones of a sensitive soul's discernment of the holiness of his God are present as he sings,

Let him that glorieth glory in this, that he hath understanding and knowledge of me, that I am Jehovah who executeth lovingkindness, justice, and righteousness in the earth, for *in these things I delight,* saith Jehovah (9:24).

Underlying Jeremiah's fierce denunciation of his people's sins and his confident predictions of national disaster is this fundamental conception of God. God cannot do anything else. He is a holy God and therefore cannot regard sin lightly. Here is no soft, easy, sentimental idea of God, but the knowledge of a God great enough in His essential being to command the awe and reverence of mankind. Sin is abhorrent because God is righteous. Sin is destructive because it is a violation of that fundamental integrity which is the essence of God and which He has built into the very structure of His creation. Reading such lofty declarations as 6:11, 12:1 ff., 17:10, and especially the prophetic picture in 33: 14, 15, of Jeremiah's covenant-keeping God, one hears a reverent hymn throughout the book proclaiming the praise of a holy God:

> God the all-righteous One, man hath defied Thee!
> Yet to eternity standeth Thy Word;
> Falsehood and wrong shall not tarry beside Thee;
> Give to us peace in our time, O Lord!

One sees a great soul bowing in the presence of Him who fills all the heavens and earth and hears as in anticipation a Sanctus ascending:

> Holy, Holy, Holy, Lord God of Sabaoth,
> Heaven and earth are full of Thy glory.

"MERCY AND TRUTH ARE MET TOGETHER"

The question of the Philippian jailer to St. Paul, "What must I do to be saved?" expresses the deepest craving of man's soul. The jailer was not, when he asked it, seeking the kind of salvation the Apostle invited him to receive. But the words and form of his speech declare the universal quest of man. The religions and philosophies outside the Hebrew-Christian theology have little of hope or encouragement to offer in answer to this quest. Possibly the chief reason for this is that their systems find it difficult to include the idea of mercy in their concept of the rule of the universe. A teacher once said, "Can God forgive sins? I do not know that God has the right to forgive sins. For a sinful man to approach a righteous God is like climbing marble stairs heated white hot." His insight was true. There is no salvation, no possibility of release, if there is no place in the rule of life for the quality of mercy. And this quality is found in its highest expression in the Christian religion and the Hebrew faith from which it stemmed.

It is not always clearly discerned in the Old Testament economy. Many readers of the pre-Christian literature profess to find in it justice, holiness, truth, and providence, but little of mercy.

When men discount the mercy of the Old Testament, however, they have not interpreted its message faithfully. To be sure, the great seers and spokesmen of Israel do not know the grace of God as it comes to its full flowering in the religion of the New Testament. "In the beginning was the Word . . . and the Word was God. And the Word" (which was God) "became flesh and dwelt among us; and we beheld His glory, glory as of the only begotten from the Father, full of *grace* and truth." This revelation of grace had not yet been given its winsome incarnation. The grace of God, that positive, active, outreaching of God's love which loves men and seeks their salvation regardless of, in spite of, their unlovely lack of merit, is a mystery as great as the Being of God himself. Only in the Incarnation, culminating with the redemptive act of the Cross, can men begin to see the grace of God. As W. A. Smart has said, "The atoning death of Jesus stands for something deeper than we will ever perfectly understand, for it stands for something in the heart of God. But at least we can see one clear and steady ray of light shining from the Cross, and that ray reveals the fact that this redemption—this rescue from evil—was achieved at the cost of suffering."[2]

Mercy is the clemency bestowed by the offended upon the offender. It may be bestowed willingly or grudgingly. It remits the punishment that is due the guilty.

A story is told that as Napoleon rode through the Rue Rivoli at the head of a triumphant procession, a young girl threw herself before his horse, crying out, "Mercy, mercy!" Napoleon, halting, commanded her to rise, and asked her, "For whom do you seek mercy?" "For my father," was her reply. "He is the officer you ordered to be shot for treason." The general's face hardened as he said, "Your father shall have justice." Vehemently she renewed her plea, exclaiming, "Not justice! That means death. Not justice; mercy, sire. Mercy!"

It is conceivable that Napoleon, moved by the emotional plea and the importunate cry of the maid, could have remitted the penalty. He could have decreed, perhaps grudgingly, that the law should not take its course. That would have been mercy; but grace is a different quality. It is the outflowing of a love which just because it is love initiates the search for the recovery and employs every means for the restoration of the offending and lost soul. It is the shepherd actively seeking the sheep that has strayed. It is the "Hound of Heaven" pursuing the fleeing sinner with love's pursuit. It is the father welcoming and restoring the returning prodigal. It is the sovereign beseeching his rebellious sub-

---

[2] *The Contemporary Christ* (New York: Abingdon-Cokesbury Press) p. 157.

jects through his ambassador to be reconciled to him. It is
the Son of God emptying himself and becoming obedient
unto death, even the death of the Cross. This grace is foreshadowed throughout the Old Testament. It is seen in its
fullness only in Christ, "Ye know the grace of our Lord
Jesus Christ."

But if the grace of God is not disclosed in its full-orbed
beauty in the Old Testament, the mercy of God is not absent
from its pages. And Jeremiah is one of the great voices proclaiming it. The God of Jeremiah was a God of mercy.
Though he perceived so clearly the justice and holiness of
God that his pictures of an avenging Deity seem almost distorted, he was able also to say, "With the Lord there is
mercy," and this was not a dim, vague apprehension for him.
It was a burning conviction that flashed out repeatedly in his
messages. Like the psalmist he saw that in his God "mercy
and truth are met together; righteousness and peace have
kissed each other" (Ps. 85:10).

Backsliding Israel hath showed herself more righteous than
treacherous Judah. . . . Return, thou backsliding Israel . . . I
will not look upon thee in anger, *for I am merciful*, saith Jehovah.
I will not keep anger forever (3:11, 12).

Reading this entire section we are impressed with one inescapable fact. We who so often think of and proclaim a cheap
repentance—a religion that, to use Hubert Simpson's phrase,
is "drained of sacrifice and drenched with sentiment"—see in
the message of Jeremiah the theme of costly repentance and
a mercy that is correspondingly real and precious. "But I
said, how will I put thee among the children and give thee a
goodly heritage of the hosts of the nations! And I said, ye
shall call me My Father and shall not turn away from follow-

ing me. . . . A voice is heard upon the bare heights, the weeping and the supplications of the children of Israel because they have perverted their ways, they have forgotten Jehovah their God. Return, ye backsliding children. I will heal your backslidings" (3:19-22).

Not once, but many times, especially in his earlier messages, the prophet returns to his theme. If the people will repent and turn to God and the ways of God, He will pardon and heal them. He sees deliverance and restoration for the nation until he is finally convinced that actual reformation is no longer possible. Until that conviction becomes fixed, however, he proclaims the possibility if the condition of receiving it is fulfilled. Even as he predicts disaster and defeat he sees the possibility of revival and health. "I will pluck them up from off their land, and will pluck up the house of Judah from among them. And it shall come to pass that after I have plucked them up, I will return and have compassion upon them" (12:15).

That reality of which the Christian hymn sings—the double cure—salvation and cleansing, is woven as a thread into the fabric of his religious conception. His God will not only forgive the sin, that is, remit the penalty. He will cleanse and heal the life of the transgressor. "I will restore health upon thee. I will heal thee of thy wounds" (30:17). And this passage sings its word of hope which through the ages has comforted the souls of men: "Ye shall be my people and I will be your God" (30:22).

The Gospel according to St. Luke gives us that matchless story of the way of God with the lost soul. Christian thought has dwelt so intensively upon the experience of the lost soul that it has almost overlooked the intention of Jesus to give men a picture of the heart of the Father. It is in common speech the "Parable of the Prodigal Son." But in the purpose of Jesus it is the eternal picture of God the Father of all sinning children.

In the Old Testament there is little presentation of God as Father. Not until Jesus came and taught men to lift their eyes to heaven and pray "Our Father" did men dare think of themselves in so close a relation to God. But Jeremiah has in one of his tenderest passages presented to us an unforgettable picture of the prodigal's Father,

They shall come with weeping, and with supplication will I lead them. I will cause them to walk by rivers of waters in a straight way wherein they shall not stumble; for I am a father to Israel, and Ephraim is my first-born son (31:9).

Is Ephraim my dear son? Is he a darling child? For as often as I speak to him I do earnestly remember him still: therefore my heart yearneth for him; I will surely have mercy upon him, saith Jehovah (31:20).

Any adequate picture of Jeremiah's God must include the word with which this chapter begins: "I have loved thee with an everlasting love" (31:3).

Victor Hugo in *Les Miserables* pictures the old priest, the Bishop Bienvenu, after a wearying day. He is writing a note, the reflection of his day's experience. And this is the note: "O Thou that art! Ecclesiastes calls Thee Omnipotent; the Maccabees call Thee Creator; the Epistle to the Ephesians calls Thee Liberty; Baruch calls Thee Immensity; the Psalms call Thee Wisdom and Truth; St. John calls Thee Light; the Book of Kings calls Thee Lord; Exodus calls Thee Providence; Leviticus, Holiness; Esdras, Justice; Creation calls Thee God; man calls Thee Father; but Solomon calls Thee Mercy, and that is the fairest of all Thy names." Jeremiah

94

too, who knew God so well as Creator, as Justice, and as Holiness, knew Him also by the fairest of all His names, Mercy.

"Spirit With Spirit Can Meet"

"Speak, Lord, for Thy servant heareth," the youthful Samuel was commanded by Eli to say, as God called him to his notable career. The counsel was based upon the truth that the God of Israel is One who enters into personal fellowship with His children. He is not an impersonal force, supremely great, ruling the universe. He is not an awesome person, remote from the life of man. He is the God of Abraham, of Isaac, and of Jacob. That is, He is a personal God. "Spirit with spirit can meet."

Most pronounced upon the pages of Jeremiah—indeed vital for any understanding of his prophetic career—is this conception of personal communion between God and man. The God of Jeremiah was One with whom the soul of man had actual transactions. The first three chapters tell the story of the meeting between God and His chosen vessel—God confronting man and man responding. "Before thou camest forth from the womb, I sanctified thee. . . . I have appointed thee a prophet to the nations" (1:5). God was the Initiator in this matter of the career of Jeremiah. He moved into the life of the chosen man of Anathoth, and actively took direction over him. When the disciples of Jesus felt their insufficiency for the task to which they were called, His word to them was: "Ye have not chosen me, I have chosen you and appointed you." And when Jeremiah quailed before his mission the word of the Lord came to him: "I am with thee to deliver thee. . . . I have made thee a fortified city, and an iron pillar, and brazen walls" (1:8, 18).

The reality of this fellowship appears in the very language

with which the prophet carries his perplexities to God. He argues the case when his mind cannot encompass the problems with which life besets him.

Righteous art thou, O Jehovah, when I contend with thee. Yet would I reason the cause with thee. Wherefore doth the way of the wicked prosper? (12:1).

"Thou hast deceived me, and I was deceived" (20:7). The word "patah," which has been variously translated, means "to be simple, easily persuaded, duped, beguiled, deceived." It speaks of an intimate, direct, personal relationship. Jeremiah's complaint has this sort of personal transaction back of it. His God is the kind of God to whom a man may lay bare the innermost recesses of his soul, whose counsel may be sought in the daily problems of life, with whom the heart of a perplexed man may find a meeting place.

One of the revealing pictures of Jeremiah's God is that in the eleventh chapter, when the prophet reminds the people of God's hand in their history and represents Him entreating the rebellious nation. "For I earnestly protested unto your fathers in the day that I brought them up out of the land of Egypt unto this day rising early and protesting saying, Obey my voice" (11:7). In Jeremiah we see a foregleam of that message which became clearly vocal in the man laid hold upon by the living Christ, "We are ambassadors therefore, as though God were entreating by us; be ye reconciled to God" (II Cor. 5:20).

Throughout that collection of verse previously referred to as "The Confessions of Jeremiah" there runs the record of a man's conversations with God which have about them the fragrance of intimate friendship. At the funeral service of Bishop Thoburn of the Methodist Church his brother related the story of a conversation which occurred once on shipboard between the bishop and several atheistically inclined ladies. These ladies had spent several hours each day presenting to him the case for atheism. Finally, as the voyage neared its end, one of them said to him: "Bishop, we are concerned to know whether our logic has made any impression upon you." He replied, "Ladies, I have enjoyed our conversations greatly. Seldom have I heard a more cogent presentation of a cause. But I assure you that I have enjoyed the conversations purely as an intellectual exercise. There was no more likelihood of your convincing me of the nonexistence of God than of the nonexistence of myself. You see, for forty years *I have known* Him."

Jeremiah's finest verses disclose just such a personal knowledge of God. A God whom he has known many years speaks through the prophet's lines: "Am I a God afar off? Can any hide himself in a secret place and I not see him? saith Jehovah. Do not I fill heaven and earth?" (23:23, 24).

Every man's God is faithfully disclosed in his praying. Samson's final prayer in the temple of the Philistines for one more flash of strength that vengeance may fall upon his tormentors is a revelation, not only of Samson but of the kind of God in whom he believes. The Pharisee's prayer, full of pride of self and class confidence, is a picture of the Pharisee's God. Jesus praying on the Cross, with that grace of the "sandalwood tree which blesses with its fragrance the axe that smites it": "Father forgive them" discloses the God of His soul's devotion.

There is one striking scene in the Book of Jeremiah which lets us see a prophet at prayer. In this scene the mind and spirit of Jeremiah are uncovered, so that the witness of it feels that here is faithful testimony concerning the worshiper's God. After the transaction with his cousin Hanamel, when Jeremiah risked his money on his faith in the word of the Lord and bought the property in Anathoth, the prophet was depleted physically and spiritually. The whole transaction was a venture of faith. Imprisoned, despised, and apparently beaten, he was challenged to take a tangible risk, to dare something for his faith. He did so only after a costly struggle. And as the reaction from that conflict swept over him, he sought release and renewal in prayer. Tracing the prophet's outpouring of spirit in his prayer, the reader sees clearly delineated the kind of God whom Jeremiah knew as reality. And the God thus disclosed is the Almighty Maker of heaven and earth (32:17). He is the All-Righteous (18, 19). He is the Ruler of destinies (20-24). And He is the All-Merciful One (18). But the picture is not complete in only these details. One who marks the burden of this great soul's prayer must be profoundly impressed by the fact that to Jeremiah God is the kind of personal friend to whom a man can take such transactions as the purchase of a field, especially if the purchase is an act of confidence in the integrity of God. He is the God to be found and communed with not only in the places and times and experiences conventionally regarded as religious, but also in the daily, commonplace experiences of this present world. The God thus known and experienced rules, directs, and transfigures, not one compartment of life but the whole of life itself. God, prayer, and human relationships could be expressed for Jeremiah in the moving verse of Archbishop Trench:

If we with earnest effort could succeed
To make our life one long connected prayer

As lives of some perhaps have been and are;
If never leaving Thee, we had no need
Our wandering spirits back again to lead
Into Thy presence, but continue there,
Like angels standing on the topmost stair
Of the sapphire throne—that were to pray indeed.

Jeremiah on the Worship of God

And chiefly Thou, O Spirit, that dost prefer
Before all temples the upright heart and pure,
Instruct me, for Thou know'st, Thou from the first
Wast present, and, with mighty wings outspread,
Dovelike sat'st brooding on the vast Abyss,
And mad'st it pregnant: what in me is dark
Illumine, what is low raise and support;
That to the highth of this great argument
I may assert Eternal Providence
And justify the ways of God to men.

     —*Paradise Lost*, Book 1, JOHN MILTON

Across the centuries Jeremiah and John Milton strike hands. Akin in spirit, they discern the true nature of spiritual worship. Interpreters of the ways of God to men, they both perceive that "the Most High dwelleth not in temples made with hands." They meet on common ground in the dissatisfaction they share with a religious worship blind to the truth that God is Spirit and "prefers before all temples the upright heart and pure."

From the human point of view the prophet's dissatisfaction with his people's worship of God is difficult to understand. His earliest association with religion was with that kind of worship which men are often wont to praise, a worship that has graduated from its narrow provincial forms and

100

has assimilated elements from various cultures. He grew up in the midst of a people who were like the Athenians, whom St. Paul described as "very religious." They had altars and shrines upon every hilltop. They retained their veneration for the God of their fathers. But they mingled with their worship of Him the customs and practices derived from the culture of older civilizations.

This synthesis of religions, so admirable and desirable to many thinkers, ancient and modern, failed to satisfy Jeremiah. From it he moved into an experience with a practice of religion that, externally at least, promised to be ideal. Reforms of the most exalted character swept away the accretions of the years and recovered elements that were fundamental to Hebrew faith and practice. Pagan gods were banished. The shrines and groves and altars of the alien deities were abolished. "One God, one temple, one word," the God of Abraham, Isaac, and Jacob, the temple at Jerusalem, and the Deuteronomic Code, these were made supreme and central.

Yet even this reformed, purified system failed to satisfy the clear-eyed young man of priestly descent in Anathoth. There was yet something lacking. It was against this very system, as much as against the idolatries, that his life was poured out in unflagging protest. And this is significant and most revealing. Among the Hebrew prophets, the greatest, the most spiritually discerning, were profoundly aware that the experience of a vital religion is more than belief in God, more than performing a ritual. It is the meeting of spirit with spirit. It is having actual transactions with the Infinite. True religion has its roots in worship. It begins with the soul's fellowship with God. It matures and flourishes and ripens through continuing in His presence. The most potent

101

assault upon religion is not the convincing logic of the atheist. It is the perversion or prevention of sincere worship. He who would destroy religion may dispense with the atheistic argument and antireligious propaganda while he centers his assault upon the believer's fellowship with God. Antireligious regimes, as Russian Communism and Hitlerian Nazism, displayed a shrewd wisdom in organizing the industrial and recreational life of their people so that the hours of common worship were pre-empted. What arguments could not accomplish, the strangling of corporate fellowship did. For the true life of religion in all its aspects flowers from the act of worship. That prophet, therefore, contributes most to a total religious conception of life who speaks with clearest voice upon this theme. In this Jeremiah is not the least of all the prophets. His own devotional life was so rich, his discernment of the nature and implications of the spiritual worship of God was so clear and so abundantly expressed that his testimony is peculiarly valuable.

This testimony is presented not as a specific section, distinct and entitled, but as a pervasive quality of all of Jeremiah's writings. He does not, for example, set himself to the task of writing a treatise on the worship of God, or of outlining in any given passage the rubrics of worship. His contribution to the believer's concept of worship is woven as a component element into all the product of his mind and pen. It is to be discerned in every section of his work. And its chief instruction and inspiration are to be found by viewing it in the light of the total situation, political, moral, and religious, to which he addressed himself. In two vital areas this contribution is timely and impressive. The voice of Jeremiah was lifted powerfully and effectively for a recovery of:

Singleness and Spirituality In Worship[1]

When the Hebrew nation came into being and received the charter of its true life, two great words stood at its beginning, "Thou shalt have no other gods before me" and "Thou shalt not make unto thee any graven image." God alone was to be worshiped without a rival. And God was to be worshiped in spirit and in truth. The first commandment is really two commands: "Hear, O Israel, the Lord thy God is one God; and thou shalt worship the Lord thy God, and Him only shalt thou serve." Fundamental to the true life of the nation was the demand for singleness in worship. But side by side with that duty was the demand that the worship of this one God be kept spiritual in its character. Peril to the religious life threatened not only from the multiplication of deities, but from the loss of a spiritual concept of the one God. The Lord Jehovah could be worshiped as the only God of the Hebrew people. And yet He could be worshiped unworthily through images that would degrade and distort His essentially spiritual nature. God could be lost as well through the device created to visualize Him as through the enthronement of other deities. And, as though recognizing the threat that down through the years would come from both these quarters, the first commandment thundered its demand for "singleness and spirituality" in worship.

Jeremiah, therefore, went back to fundamentals in his emphasis. With unflagging zeal he pleaded for a recovery of these two qualities. With stern vehemence he assailed his people's departures from the basic demands of their religion. His first complaint was directed against their loss of singleness in worship.

---

[1] The phrase is derived from Dr. Cleland B. McAfee's treatment of the Commandments in *The Mosaic Law and Modern Life*.

103

"I will utter my judgments against them touching all their wickedness in that they have forsaken me and burned incense to other gods and have worshiped the works of their own hands" (1:16).

In one telling word the prophet summarized the double failure. But chiefly it was against their multiplicity of deities that he cried out. This was at the start of his prophetic career when the many shrines testified to the divided loyalties of the people. In essence these people were worshiping that which would insure their prosperity. The central symbols and images of the pagan cults were those which signified fertility, expressive of the desire of men to have from their religion as its chief fruit a prosperous life, fertile fields, large families, and all the material goals that men have immemorially coveted. The Hebrew people drew into their religious practices the rites of the pagans, partly because of the seductive appeal of their sensual and lascivious accompaniments, but chiefly because they hoped thus to insure their own prosperity.

Repeatedly throughout the preaching of Jeremiah there appears his impatience with the proneness of men to divide the loyalty of their hearts between Jehovah, their God, and the deities of the peoples about them.

The lack of unity in their thought of God, and the accompanying confusion of life, overwhelm him as he exclaims, "As many as thy cities in number, So many, O Judah, thy gods" (2:28, 11:13; tr. by George Adam Smith). His conflict rose to its most dramatic proportions near the end of his career in an incident full of significance for the religious life of any age. Deep disaster had overtaken the people of Judah. The force of Josiah's reforms had spent itself, and the people had lapsed into the old idolatries. Jeremiah's worst predictions had been fulfilled. Jerusalem was a broken city, and the remnant had gone into Egypt. There they succumbed to the old appeal of religion as a prosperity device. They burned incense to the queen of heaven. And in Jeremiah's denunciation of their apostasy, as well as in their reply, is disclosed a conception of religious motive that has always imperiled worship.

Thus saith Jehovah of hosts, the God of Israel: ye have seen all the evil that I have brought upon Jerusalem and upon all the cities of Judah: and behold, this day they are a desolation . . . because of their wickedness which they have committed to provoke me to anger, in that they went to burn incense and to serve other gods, that they knew not, neither they nor their fathers. Howbeit I sent unto you all my servants, the prophets, rising up early and sending them saying, "O do not this abominable thing that I hate." . . . Therefore now thus saith Jehovah, the God of hosts, the God of Israel: Wherefore commit ye this evil against your own souls to cut off from you man and woman, infant and suckling, out of the midst of Judah! . . . in that ye provoke me unto anger with the works of your hands, burning incense unto other gods in the land of Egypt whither ye have gone to sojourn? (44:2-8).

After the prophet had delivered his message excoriating the people who forsook the God of their fathers, they made their memorable reply:

We will certainly perform every word that is gone forth out of our mouth, to burn incense unto the queen of heaven and to pour out drink offerings unto her, as we have done, we and our fathers, our kings and our princes, in the cities of Judah and in the streets of Jerusalem; for then we had plenty of victuals, and were well, and saw no evil. But since we left off burning incense unto the queen of heaven and pouring out drink offerings unto her, we have wanted all things and have been consumed by the sword and by the famine (44:17, 18).

Here is the classic picture of a religion which is in its essence a prosperity cult. Its devotees declare frankly that they worship as they do because they believe that it pays. They are the descendants of a people who were willing to give up the adventure with God in a Promised Land to go back into slavery because they could not forget the fleshpots of Egypt. They are the forebears of a people whose eager self-interest prompted Jesus to say, "Ye sought me not because ye saw signs, but because ye did eat and were filled." They are typical of all those in all ages who seek Him not for His own sake but for the loaves and the fishes, and who justify the cynical sneer of Satan: "Doth Job serve God for naught?"

"No Other Gods Before Me" was the title of the sermon Jeremiah unceasingly preached to this kind of people. It is the text of the sermon he continues to preach to the people of God in every age. For however scornful modern man may be of these ancient worshipers who burned incense to the queen of heaven, he may well ask to what gods of prosperity he burns incense. Seldom is the motive of self-interest so frankly acknowledged as in the speech of these refugees in Egypt: "We will continue to burn incense to the queen of heaven as we formerly did; for then we had plenty to eat, were well, and saw no evil." The motive itself has never entirely disappeared. Religion has continued to be conceived in terms of prosperous circumstance. "I will praise the Lord because he hath dealt bountifully with me," say the comfortable devotees of a religion whose forms they continue to observe because they feel vaguely that their personal good fortune, or their national victory and prosperous estate, are bound up with keeping this worship alive. God ceases to be

106

the One in whom the soul loses itself and becomes the One who can bestow the fatness of life.

That is a telling description of this type of religious devotion which Henry Van Dyke gives in his story, "The Mansion." Mr. Weightman, wealthy patron of the benevolent and philanthropic enterprises of his community, as well as senior warden of St. Petronius Church, is counseling his son against a certain altruistic adventure. The father is conservative and calculating even in his charities. He is the kind of man who contributes to foreign missions because he has understood that the missionaries do a great deal to open the door to foreign trade. The son desires to enlist his father's assistance on behalf of a college classmate who needs medical care and a period of rest in Colorado. He wants for himself the parental consent and assistance as he goes to Labrador to labor with Grenfell among the fishermen. The father urges that these are not rewarding enterprises. They are hidden and lost in obscurity. All of his own charities bear the family name and bring the reward of distinction and opportunity to the benefactor. The son had once said, "It sounds like cant, I know, but sometimes I feel as if I'd like to do some good in the world if father only wouldn't insist upon God's putting it into the ledger." Now, impatient as his father's self-interested motive impresses itself upon him, he exclaims, "I can see it already, sir, and the way you describe it looks amazingly wise and prudent. In other words, we must cast our bread upon the waters in large loaves, carried by sound ships marked with the owner's name, so that the return freight will be sure to come back to us."[2]

Incense is burned to the queen of heaven not only in

_____
[2] "The Mansion," in *The Unknown Quantity*, pp. 332, 339.

Egypt by an ancient people but in many a modern church and by worshipers whose essential motive differs little from that so baldly declared by Jeremiah's people. The idea of serving God for His own sake and not for the blessings He can bestow, or following Christ for His divine grace, and not for the loaves and the fishes, seems strange and unreal. The worshipers of the queen of heaven cannot understand Francis Xavier as he sings:

> O God, I love Thee; not that my poor love
> May win me entrance to Thy heaven above,
> Nor yet that strangers to Thy love must know
> The bitterness of everlasting woe.

> How can I choose but love Thee, God's dear Son,
> O Jesus, loveliest and most loving One!
> Were there no heaven to gain, no hell to flee,
> For what Thou art alone I must love Thee.

> Not for the hope of glory or reward,
> But even as Thyself hast loved me, Lord,
> I love Thee and will love Thee and adore,
> Who art my King, my God, forevermore.

Jeremiah's warfare in the area of his people's worship was not limited to the effort to preserve their singleness of devotion. This battle he fought with an intensity that could be termed intolerance. He insisted that the deities of the pagans were "no gods." Jehovah could be God only if there were no other gods to divide the loyalty of men's hearts. But the prophet contended just as earnestly against the insistent tendency of men to degrade their idea of God to the level of an image. Even while the command to preserve spirituality in worship was being given to Moses in the mount, the people, just delivered from the slavery of Egypt, resorted to the image as their means of worship. Repeatedly throughout their history they lapsed into this practice. It was the accompaniment of their declining spiritual sense of God and of their divided religious loyalty. Jeremiah came into his ministry just when this practice was at its height. He was aroused to some of his most vehement denunciations by it. What is perhaps his finest satire, that in the tenth chapter, was inspired by this spiritual obtuseness. This passage has been reviewed in another section. Here it is sufficient to note the scorn of the prophet for the impotence of the image,

They fasten it with nails and hammers that it *move not*. They are like a palm tree, of turned work, and *speak not*. They *cannot go* . . . they cannot do evil, neither is it in them to do good (10:4, 5).

The God of Jeremiah was living, active, powerful. One of the most vital elements of his concept of God was His living quality. "Jahwe that doeth it," "I am awake," "Shall I not visit," were Jeremiah's characteristic phrases to describe his God. Against the background of this idea of God the biting sarcasm of the prophet's satire stands out in boldest relief.

The temple sermon with its solemn warning, "Say not, the temple, the temple, the temple, amend your ways, execute righteousness, oppress not," was preached to a people living complacently in the belief that God is worshiped if only the proper symbols, the sacred places, and the traditional forms and ceremonies are preserved and venerated. In the bold, eloquent plea of this dramatic message Jeremiah declared his conviction that no image or institution may be permitted to intrude itself between the worshiper and God. He restated for his own age that truth which the reformers of every age have recovered and applied to their generations, the truth of

109

the soul's direct access to God. The religion of the spirit was his theme. He announced in his own way that truth to which Jesus was destined to give epoch-making expression, "God is a spirit, and they that worship him must worship him in spirit and in truth" (John 4:24).

The second area in which Jeremiah makes a significant contribution to the believer's understanding of the worship of God is:

ACHIEVING REALITY IN WORSHIP

One word which more completely than any other fits Jeremiah's whole religious concept is the word *reality*. It stands forcefully in the midst of the verses (18:13-15) in which he indicts his people for their loss of integrity. "They serve the unreal." Unreal worship was to him the spring whence flowed all the evils that assailed and possessed the life of the nation.

It is possible to trace very accurately the elements by which Jeremiah achieved reality in worship and thus to discern his chief contribution to religious thought on this vital subject.

The reader of his literature, particularly the devotional sections, cannot fail to be impressed by the prophet's:

AWARENESS AND CONFESSION OF SIN
Hear and give ear and be not proud!
For Jahwe hath spoken.
Give Jahwe your God the glory
Ere it grow dark:
Before your feet stumble
On darkening mountains,
And you wait for light, but darkness is there,
And he turns it to gloom.
—13:15, 16; tr. by John Skinner

110

Pride must go or God will go, the prophet seems to be saying to an age which has apparently forgotten how to humble itself before the Most High God, and has trusted in its own wisdom and resources. He pleads persistently for that humbleness of spirit which stands at the door of entrance into the heavenly kingdom. He renounces all self-trust and makes simple and sincere confession of sin both for himself and the nation.

> If our offences witness against us, Jahwe,
> Act for Thine own name's sake!
> For many are our backslidings before Thee,
> Against Thee have we sinned.
>
> Thou Hope of Israel, Jahwe
> Its Saviour in time of need!
> Why be like a guest in the land,
> As a traveler spending the night?
>
> Why be like a man asleep
> As one unable to save?
> For Thou'rt in our midst, O Jahwe,
> By Thy name are we called
> Forsake us not quite!
>
> —14:7-9; tr. by John Skinner

At the basis of any real communion with God, before the reality begins, there stands the humble and contrite heart. There is that sincere acknowledgment of need so lacking in the Laodicean Church, so acute in the Fifty-first Psalm, so foreign to the Pharisee—"God, I thank thee that I am not like other men," so real to the publican—"God, be merciful to me a sinner." Opening the door to God begins with the spirit that sings in Cornelius Elven's hymn:

111

With broken heart and contrite sigh,
A trembling sinner, Lord, I cry;
Thy pardoning grace is rich and free;
O God, be merciful to me!

Jeremiah prays in this spirit: "We acknowledge, O Jehovah, our wickedness, and the iniquity of our fathers: for we have sinned against thee" (14:20). "We have sinned!" That simple, sincere sentence is about the most difficult thing men have to say. It holds, however, the promise of health for the individual or the nation. Its absence is the portent of failure.

Earlier prophets than Jeremiah perceived this and sounded the call for a thoroughgoing repentance. Hosea, the prophet of the God of love and mercy, became sarcastic as he caricatured his people's shallow repentance. "Come and let us return unto Jehovah; for he hath torn and he will heal us; he hath smitten, and he will bind us up. After two days he will revive us; on the third day he will raise us up. . . . O Ephraim . . . your goodness is as the morning cloud, and as the dew that goeth early away" (Hos. 6:1-4). It was just in this easygoing conception of God, and light view of sin, that Jeremiah saw a threatening peril. His scorn for shallow repentance seems to have taken fire from the spirit of Hosea. Smith's translation of two of his speeches makes this vivid:

They would heal the breach of My people
As though it were trifling,
Saying, "It is well, it is well—"
When—where is it well?
                    —6:14; tr. by George Adam Smith

Not a man repents of his evil
Saying, "What have I done?"
                    —8:6, *ibid*

112

A broken, defeated people like the Judah of Jeremiah's day, or the Germany of today, may be induced to say with sincerity, "We have sinned." Proud, victorious people are not likely to be aware of the need for saying it. One who studies the moods and attitudes and movements of the victorious nations since 1945 may readily discern the applicability of Jeremiah's word to a day like this, and to the children of this age.

Indeed, one of the most disquieting manifestations of the life of the world at this moment is the evident lack of any sense of shortcoming, personal or corporate. In Erich Remarque's book, *The Road Back*, there is a revealing section in which he discusses education in Germany after World War I. He and his comrades who had experienced defeat on the field returned expecting to find in the classrooms of their schools a changed attitude from the old shibboleths, reliances, and complacency which they felt had led them into disaster. They looked for a repentant attitude and the birth of a new spirit. In short, they hoped to find that humble and contrite heart which to them would be the promise of a new and better world. Instead they found the old arrogance, pride, and hatreds. Teachers apparently were intent upon going back to an old life and were not aware of any need for renunciation and contrition. And the thoughtful among those returning, defeated warriors faced the future disillusioned and with grave forebodings in their hearts.

The testimony of this section is significant and ought to be instructive for the world situation today. Possibly it was this portion of his work with its plea for a contrite heart that more than anything else caused the author to be banished from a Germany resurgent with nationalistic ambitions. Certainly it was the nation that rejected such a plea which

113

marched down the road that led to the global disaster resultant in its own dismemberment.

But it must not be supposed that this need is a need for one nation only. It is an even more urgent need for the people and the nations upon whose banners victory alighted. As Mazzini, the Italian patriot, once said, "The morrow of victory is always more perilous than its eve." Among these people not many voices are heard saying, "We have sinned." On the contrary every major effort is made to establish officially the guilt of the defeated, and even the most mild suggestion of mutual failure is received with scorn and derision. In all the councils of the statesmen of victorious nations there is no disposition actually to turn away from the devices and reliances, from the machinery and arrangements, that through the ages have contributed to the same fatal result. The very insistence upon fixing the sole guilt for the disaster upon the defeated builds up the pride and confidence of the victorious. And today a world organization of victors finds difficulty in functioning largely because it has not yet discerned the need for turning away from the pride, selfishness, and ambition that have ever been the foes of world co-operation.

For this very moment in world history, as for every critical period, Jeremiah has a vital word: "We acknowledge our wickedness—for we have sinned," this prophet confesses sincerely. And in his confession he is standing very near to the kingdom of God. He is manifesting the spirit that Jesus required for entrance to the heavenly kingdom when He took a child and placed him in the midst of His disciples as symbol of the spirit that must rule those who enter His spiritual kingdom. This is the first element of Jeremiah's achievement of reality in worship.

114

Equally evident in the devotional literature of Jeremiah is his:

FELLOWSHIP AND COMMUNION WITH GOD

This prophet had actual transactions with the Infinite. He spoke with God, and the record of his speaking with God displays a remarkable characteristic. One cannot but be impressed by the manner in which Jeremiah carried to God the problems of his everyday life. No occurrence was too trivial for him to make a subject of prayer. He talked to God as to a familiar friend. And yet one feels the sense of awe which breathes through all his communion. He never failed to take the shoes from off his feet as one who knows that when he is in the presence of God he stands on holy ground. Even his disputes with God when the mood of rebellion possessed him combine with the protest an underlying sense of reverence that cannot be wholly hid.

We have many records of Jeremiah's actual communion with God. His prayer life is an open book. The section which contains his devotional poetry is a remarkably fine picture of a great soul in the practice of prayer. And through it all there breathes the sense of awe, of holy mystery, the deep reverence of one who is aware that his dealings are with the Most High.

> But to me is Thy word a delight,
> The joy of my heart;
> For Thy name has been named upon me
> O Jahwe of Hosts.
>
> —15:16; tr. by John Skinner

> Deep beyond sounding is the heart
> And sick beyond cure:
> Who can know it?
> I, Jahwe, search the heart

And try the reins
To give to a man as his ways
The fruit of his doings.
                    —17:9, 10; tr. by John Skinner

One of the passages most expressive of this high communion is the prayer recorded in the thirty-second chapter, after Jeremiah's venture of faith.

Ah Lord, Jahweh, behold thou hast made the heavens and the earth by thy great power, and by thine outstretched arm. Nothing is too hard for thee who showed loving-kindness unto thousands and recompensed the iniquities of the fathers into the bosom of their children: the great, the mighty God, Jehovah of hosts is his name; great in counsel and mighty in work . . . who didst set signs and wonders in the land of Egypt even unto this day, and madest thee a name (32:16 ff.).

As one reads with sympathetic understanding this outpouring of the prophet's spirit one is aware of a great soul treading in awe in the presence of the majesty of the Lord of heaven and earth. His prayer administers a rebuke to our selfish prayers that are so abounding in petition and so barren of adoration. One is made to think of that picture of another great spirit at prayer, St. Francis of Assisi, as he kneels all night before the altar repeating with utmost reverence the single word, "God!" One hears Frederick W. Faber's hymn of holy adoration ascending:

> My God! how wonderful Thou art,
> Thy majesty how bright!
> How beautiful Thy Mercy-seat,
> In depths of burning light!

A final factor which contributes to the prophet's achievement of reality in worship, after his confession and communion is his:

116

Donald Hankey, "Student In Arms" of World War I, defined religious faith as "betting one's life on God." His phrase was coined no doubt in revulsion against a very common but superficial conception of faith suggested by the child's naive definition, "faith means believing what you know isn't so." It was a reaction against the idea that faith means merely intellectual assent or confessional regularity. It was an unsanctified setting for the truth which theology declares more ponderously—that faith consists of three elements, "knowledge, assent, and confidence." Faith is never true faith until it is completed in the committal of the whole life. In this sense Jeremiah was a man of faith. Throughout his entire life, at every stage of his career, the student comes upon evidence of this quality. Faith may never have been defined by him in measured terms. But no one can read the story of his life, from the record of his call, through all his struggles, down to the final ignominy of his fate, without realizing that the God he worshiped was nothing unless He was the supreme end of his devotion. He literally "bet his life on God."

One incident, typical of his whole attitude, is that recorded in Chapter 32. Jeremiah was in prison because he refused to "prophesy comfortable things" to Zedekiah. The army of the Chaldeans was threatening Jerusalem, and beginning the occupation of the land. Hanamel, the cousin of Jeremiah, came to him in prison, offering to sell him a lot in Anathoth, part of the family inheritance. His action was calculated to be a taunt to Jeremiah, to add to his discomfiture and put him in an impossible dilemma. The prophet declares that the word of the Lord had come to him counseling him that his cousin would offer him this land and advising him to purchase it, because "houses and fields and vineyards shall yet again be bought in the land."

It looked like a bad bargain. No sane person was likely to throw away perfectly good money to buy a field in Anathoth which was at that time in the hands of the invading Chaldeans. It looked as foolish, for example, as for citizens of the town of Gettysburg in July, 1863, to purchase lots along Seminary Ridge on the first day of the battle, with the Ridge in possession of the Confederate Army and its soldiers filtering into the town from the west. It was almost equivalent to being asked to buy Confederate money at face value at the close of the war between the states.

Yet Jeremiah, with every counsel of prudence against him, and while his cousin and the shrewdly wise townsfolk laughed, bought the field. He risked his money on the faith that he had in the word of the Lord that "houses and fields and vineyards would once more be bought in the land." And one of the finest pictures to speak to the imagination of men, symbol of the quality of Jeremiah's whole life of faith, is that presented by this man making his venture of faith, buying a field in his home town while the land was occupied by the enemy. A world of suggestion, widely applicable, is bound up in the simple record of verse 9, "So I bought the field that was in Anathoth of Hanamel mine uncle's son, and weighed him the money, even seventeen shekels of silver."

Not only the irreligious world, but particularly the religious world, needs to perceive the full import of this venture of faith. For there has always been some justification for the world's sneer that religion is an escape mechanism, a sort of sanctified safety-first device, cautious, prudent, expedient, guaranteed to reduce life's risks and to transport the faithful without loss of cargo to the blissful, eternal shores. From the two disciples who came to Jesus asking for the chief portfolios in the government which they expected Him to establish—"Lord, do for us," "Grant unto us"—to the most modern disciple who asks for a comfortable religion, with pleasant ministrations here and a guaranteed reward hereafter, there has always been a large admixture of sanctified self-seeking in what the world sees of our religion.

When the screen presented its dramatization of Robin Hood's adventures it included an interesting dialogue between that daring and happy warrior and the maid Marian. Robin Hood and his band had captured the henchmen of Prince John. They were being shown some of the people behind the scenes when Marian, true to her tradition, but beginning to be fascinated by the outlaw leader, asked, "But what is your reward?" And then the man who had risked death to fight treason, oppression, and injustice for the sheer joy of defeating the wrong and relieving the oppressed, looked at his questioner with poorly concealed contempt as he said, "You just can't understand." There is an attitude toward life and religion that just can't understand religion in terms of risk, adventure—"betting one's life on God."

Jeremiah, coolly paying his seventeen shekels for a field held by the enemy because "the word of the Lord" had come to him; risking tangible, valuable, visible assets for that which was out of sight, becomes a valiant symbol of religious faith at its best. His act is an everlasting rebuke to the easygoing, prudent "insurance-like" religion which is the caricature of the faith disclosed in the Scriptures. He joins hands with Abraham, leaving home and kindred and familiar associations to dwell in tents in the wilderness because he "looked for a city which hath foundations, whose builder and maker is God." He unites himself in a living fellowship with a man

119

like Moses, "choosing to endure hardship with the people of God rather than to enjoy the pleasures of sin for a season, because he endured as seeing him who is invisible." He is a living exemplar of the truth that "faith is the substance of things hoped for, the evidence of things not seen."

For Jeremiah worship and life were inseparable. Out of the experience of worship, in which reality was thus achieved, there came to him no such rewards as men have often associated with the religious life. But there did come what was for him, and must be for all discerning souls, an even richer reward. He tasted and possessed the fruits of pure worship in such inner resources as are beyond the natural mind to comprehend. One of the passages in which he testifies to the deeper satisfaction and enrichment of life is filled with suggestion for every life. "Blessed is the man that trusteth in Jehovah, and whose trust Jehovah is. For he shall be as a tree planted by the waters, that spreadeth out its roots in the river, and shall not fear when heat cometh, and its leaf shall be green; and shall not be careful in the year of drought, neither shall cease from yielding fruit" (17:7, 8).

The disciples of Jesus, returning from a visit to the markets to buy food, marveled that he seemed nourished. He replied, "I have meat to eat that ye know not of." There are inner resources, of which the world knows naught. There is sustenance for the soul, the bread of life unfailing and eternally satisfying. No prison and no adversity can take the victory out of a life sustained from within. Of this food Jeremiah was a partaker, and from it he derived a richness and fertileness of life like one of whom another psalmist sang, "And he shall be like a tree planted by the rivers of water, that bringeth forth his fruit in his season. His leaf also shall not wither" (Ps. 1:3).

Worship and Ethics

The description of a certain Victorian, that he would be equally shocked to hear Christianity questioned or to see it practiced, points to one of religion's vulnerable spots. Men have long been dividing life into compartments, and keeping its several interests—business, pleasure, politics, religion—each in its own separate cubicle, until the modern mind can ask, "Is religion relevant today?"

Jeremiah was so impressed by the decay that results when religion and life, God and His people, are separated that he resorted to a strange parable to bring the truth home to his nation.

Thus said Jehovah unto me, Go and buy thee a linen girdle, and put it upon thy loins and put it not in water. So I bought a girdle according to the word of Jehovah and put it upon my loins. And the word of Jehovah came unto me a second time saying, Take the girdle which thou hast bought, which is upon thy loins, and arise, go to the Euphrates and hide it there in a cleft of the rock. So I went and hid it by the Euphrates as Jehovah commanded me. And it came to pass after many days that Jehovah said unto me, Arise, go to the Euphrates and take the girdle from thence, which I commanded thee to hide there. Then I went to the Euphrates and digged, and took the girdle from the place where I had hid it, and behold the girdle was marred, and profitable for nothing (13:1-7).

121

The central truth of the prophet's story, the message which he sought to impress upon his people, revolves about the use made of the loin cloth. Put to the use for which it was designed, clinging close to the body of the wearer, it was a good loin cloth, a useful article. Separated from him, hidden in the earth, it became marred and decayed, "profitable for nothing." Life lived in the presence of God, in close association with Him, is good and true. The nation, made for God, clinging to Him, as the loin cloth clings closely to the wearer, fulfills its destiny and lives. Taken away from God, removed from His presence, life—whether of the individual or of the nation—becomes marred and useless. Decay is the result of the separation.

Much of Jeremiah's conflict centered about the principle involved in this parable. He found himself in the midst of a people who would have been inexpressibly shocked to hear religion, especially the religion of their reformation, questioned. They would have been equally shocked to see their religion in all its import for their life actually practiced. They attended to their religious affairs in a well-insulated compartment and transacted their business or promoted the other concerns of life in a wholly separate compartment. Looking at the nation as a whole, life in the presence of God—clinging to God in deepest reality so that the entire life was in closest touch with Him—was unknown. The incongruity between the worship life and the ethical life of the nation smote Jeremiah like a blow in the face.

"Be ye holy, even as I am holy." Inherent in the Hebrew religion and always recognized by the prophets of the spirit was the demand for a correspondence between the life of the worshiper and the moral character of the God he worshiped. True worship for these great souls was never a transaction carried on in a remote region unrelated to the life experience and life expression of the worshiper. It was an integral part of his whole life. If it failed to produce moral correspondence it ceased to be true worship.

Like all the great prophets of the spirit, Jeremiah was struck by the incongruity of a life which abounds in the forms and expressions of religious worship, yet is stranger to its power. He had only contempt for a religion that had retained the externals of its devotion, ceremonies, institutions, rituals, and had lost the vital spirit. He was tremendously aware of the ethical implications of the worship of a God who is moral character. His quarrel, sharp and intense, with his nation in this respect focused upon two phases of its life.

LIFE AND THE INSTITUTION

One of the pronounced features of Jerusalem's life, especially in the period following Josiah's reforms, was trust in the institution. It was a comfortable feeling, promoted and nurtured by the leaders, to assume that because the institution—in this case the temple—was preserved life was "ipso facto" secure. In her novel, *Inheritance*, Phyllis Bentley has a striking picture of one of humanity's perennial blind spots. The time is the period of England's industrial revolution. Machines are displacing men in the textile industry. Mill owners, greedy for profits, are blind to the human suffering this development involves. A family of industrialists, the Oldroyds, which has profited from child labor and the common exploitation of the workers, is proceeding with the installation of the feared machines. Resentment flames into open hostility, resulting in a plot by union members against the life of the head of the business. Clashes, reprisals, riots finally lead to the execution of the plot, and the death of the elder Oldroyd. His son Will, vowing vengeance, traces down the authors of the plot and secures the conviction and execution of four union members, including one innocent victim of circumstances. After the execution, horrified by the reality of it, Will makes his way across the fields through a snowstorm and turns to try to catch a glimpse of the towers of York minster. "It would be so comforting," he says, "to see the minster towers." He and his family had waxed fat and prosperous through a system that was callous to the economic injustice, the suffering, the poverty, the exploitation, it inflicted upon the underprivileged. That was a blind spot in his social vision. And in the midst of an experience, the product of it all, involving riot, bloodshed, and murder, he instinctively turned to the institution symbolized by the massive towers of York's minster, and the word that flashed into his mind was "comfort."

That is exactly the situation which Jeremiah faced. Life in all its vital expression and actual conduct was untouched and uninfluenced by the deeper realities implied in the worship of God. And the temple was so comforting. It was comforting because men had come to believe that God was localized and was bound to protect and deliver His people so long as they maintained His temple, the place of His presence. A hint of the persistence of this notion is contained in the speech of the Samaritan woman to Jesus, "Our fathers worshiped in this mountain. Ye say that Jerusalem is the place where men ought to worship." God had chosen them, they were His people; He was their champion. He must grant them victory over all their foes to vindicate their boast, "amongst the gods there is none like unto Thee." When peril threatened from without, when danger brought uneasiness within, they looked for the towers of their institution and found comfort and complacency. The temple itself created a moral blind spot. "There stands our charter of safety. The temple of Jehovah, the temple of Jehovah is this."

Intimations of this complacency-breeding doctrine are to be found throughout the preaching of the prophets. Amos put it bluntly when he voiced the complaint of God: "You only have I known of all the families of the earth: therefore will I visit upon you your iniquities" (Amos 3:2). They were hugging to themselves the blessing and privilege of their divine election. God's call to them was thought of primarily in terms of privilege. The prophet turned the thought about and bade them think of it in terms of responsibility. "You alone of all the nations has God chosen. Yes, but that does not mean that God is bound to prosper and deliver you everlastingly. You are under the responsibility of living as the people of God. The higher He has lifted you, the greater is the condemnation of your failure."

Complacency was even more pronounced in Jerusalem of Jeremiah's day. The temple was there. The beneficiaries of the temple system could be depended upon to cultivate diligently the doctrine of trust in the institution. A champion of the temple had wiped out its rivals and established its supremacy. The actual outcome of this was to create, in the thinking of the people, a responsibility for God. They spoke of "the burden of the Lord." This phrase, "Massā Yahweh," as in 23:33 ff., indicates a state of mind. An equivalent would be the modern slang expression, "It is up to God." In a crass sense they had identified the presence of their God with the visible institution. The God of the temple must now vindicate His own power and save His people. This was the burden that rested upon Him. Evidence of the impact of this assumption upon the mind of Jeremiah appears repeatedly

125

in his preaching. His rebellion against the whole pernicious development burst out in his temple sermon, one of the boldest, most scathing indictments of ecclesiasticism to be found outside the ministry and teaching of Jesus. In vivid and picturesque language the prophet challenged their divided life which permitted them to do things in the business, or the pleasure compartment that could by no means be tolerated in the religious. They were finding comfort and security in the temple, and were unrebuked by any sense of shortcoming or sin, and unaware of any threatening peril. "Nothing can happen to us," they said; "there stands our temple." Bluntly the prophet tore down this defense and stripped away the hypocrisy of it.

Amend your ways and your doings, and I will cause you to dwell in this place. Trust not in lying words, saying, The temple of Jehovah, the temple of Jehovah is this (7:3-7).

"Stop pointing to this institution," the prophet seems to say. "Find your security in a way of life and in a living fellowship with God. No institution, not even the most hallowed, can save you if your way of life defies the will of God in whose temple you trust." And then in words that literally burn he itemizes the sins that are the violation of and denial of their religion. "You pervert justice," he says. "You oppress the poor, the weak, the unprotected. You transgress the commandments of God. You steal, you commit adultery, you bear false witness. You even murder. And you do it all because you have turned away from God. You worship other gods before Him and burn incense to the graven image." The temple sermon paints, for all ages to see, a vivid picture of ecclesiasticism in its sharpest realization. Side by side with meticulous care for the establishment and strength-

126

ening of the temple of God could exist a life whose expression and occupation were the grossest violation of the very nature and revealed will of God. Let the whole temple system be as powerfully established and impregnable as it could be. It was, for Jeremiah, canceled by the fact that one could search through Jerusalem's streets for a man loving justice or practicing truth, and find none.

Ecclesiasticism, in varying expressions, has reproduced itself as the centuries have passed. Jesus faced it in a conflict that Jeremiah's battle accurately foreshadowed. The turning point of His ministry, that which crystallized the opposition, was His act of driving the buyers and sellers out of the temple. "My house shall be called a house of prayer for all people; but ye have made it a den of thieves." By Jesus' day the temple, which was designed to be the meeting place between God and man, the channel of divine truth and grace, the source and inspiration of the spiritual life, had become an institution with places, preferment, offices, emoluments, to be preserved and enjoyed. The Sadducees at this time were the chief beneficiaries of the system. They derived profit from leasing space in the temple for the stalls of those who sold to the worshipers the materials for their sacrifices, and those who changed, at a discount, their money into the temple currency. The bazaars of Annas were shrewdly exploited by the Sadducees. They became a means of oppression of the devout worshipers and of great profit to the promoters. When Jesus challenged the system, indignantly driving out the buyers and sellers, the inheritors and beneficiaries of the practice knew that something must be done. And they, who perverted the ministry of the temple with their greedy scheme, put upon the lips of their henchmen the cry, "He profanes and threatens our temple." The ecclesiastical politicians engineered Calvary. The act which forced their hand was a dramatization of that which Jeremiah had declared in the gate of the temple.

Will ye steal, murder and commit adultery, and swear falsely . . . and walk after other gods that ye have not known, and come and stand before me in this house which is called by my name and say, "We are delivered," that ye may do these abominations? Is this house which is called by my name become a den of robbers? (7:9-11).

The ecclesiastic always looks at the institution. The prophet of the spirit looks at the life. The ecclesiastic sees the institution as an end. The man of God sees it as a means to a larger end. "Build the institution, strengthen the bulwarks, look to the organization," say the ecclesiastics. "Amend your ways and your doings," say the men of God. "Strengthen and purify the life."

Visitors to the Tower of London are shown a succession of exhibits which, if the observers are thoughtful, must start them upon some significant reflections. They see the swords used by the knights upon their crusades. The weapons are ingeniously wrought with wide hilts. During the day they were wielded to inflict death upon the foes of the Church, the holders of the Holy Grail. At nightfall the soldier wiped the blood of his enemy off the blade of his great sword, thrust it into the earth, so that its hilt formed the arms of the cross. Kneeling before this cross, craving security for himself and victory over his foes, he made his prayers to the Christ who upon His cross prayed for His enemies, "Father, forgive them." On the morrow the cross once again became a sword to shed more blood for the life of the institution and the preservation of its forms.

128

Passing on, the visitors are shown the chapel with all its appointments historically and liturgically correct, and are told that here the ancient kings worshiped. The seat which Henry VIII occupied is pointed out. Devout souls, intent upon preserving the institution, were comforted by the knowledge that here, in correct symbolism, pure doctrine, and stately ritual, the temple of God was maintained. So valiantly did King Henry labor on behalf of the institution that he earned the title "Defender of the Faith." But somehow the bones that are buried beneath the dungeons will not stay out of the mind of the observer. The knowledge of political intrigue, unholy passion, schemings, divorces, and beheadings will not down. And a voice re-echoes through corridors and the correctly appointed place of prayer, "Say not, The temple, the temple; amend your ways and your doings . . . then I will cause you to dwell in this place."

"Thou hast the name of living but art dead." The message of the Spirit to the church at Sardis (Rev. 3:1) was spoken to a church which must have reproduced the situation Jeremiah faced. The institution, with all its machinery, its organizations, statistics, ritual, and external features, had the appearance of life. But like a tree which goes through the processes of the seasons, flourishes outwardly with buds and leaves but is smitten with decay at its heart, the church had only the name of living. Certain delicate fibers through which the life of God was meant to flow had begun to rot. It was perhaps stately, imposing, flourishing to the eye of man who looks upon the outward appearance, but in the eyes of God who looks upon the heart it was dead. Ceremonies without the spirit, ritual without the heart, the institution without the life—these marked the church at Sardis. These are always the marks of a dying church. It was a later reproduction of this ecclesiasticism that moved Martin Luther to pen his polemic, "The Babylonian Captivity of the Church." That church, too, had the name of living. It was powerful beyond all the dreams of a little company of first-century Christians. It was apparently living with a might never imagined in Jerusalem in the days of Herod the king. It was rich above the imagination of a man tempted to bow the knee to Satan in order to gain the kingdoms of this world. But it was actually captive in the hands of worldly-minded powers and therefore spiritually impotent. Luther's reformation blast could well have found its text in Jeremiah's temple sermon.

Jeremiah becomes especially contemporary in this phase of his struggle. Discerning eyes today cannot fail to see evidences of the threatening reproduction of the condition which has historically cast its blight upon religion. In October, 1946, Archbishop Aloysius Stepinac, primate of the Roman Catholic Church of Jugoslavia, was pronounced by a court of his land guilty of acts contrary to the government, and was summarily sentenced to imprisonment. The church almost immediately replied by excommunicating the head of the government, Marshal Tito, and all who participated in the conviction. At the same time the Congregation of the Council, disciplinary body of the church, announced a sweeping decree automatically excommunicating "anyone who brings a bishop, especially his own bishop, into a secular court; anyone who lays his hands upon a bishop or archbishop in violent manner, anyone who directly or indirectly impedes the exercise of ecclesiastical jurisdiction and in order to do so resorts to civil power."

One may be in entire sympathy with the accused bishop, and in complete opposition to the judicial procedure—with its warped standards and predetermined verdicts—of the

Communist system of which Tito is a part. One need not pronounce upon the guilt or innocence of this victim. Yet one cannot fail to see in this pronouncement of the Catholic Council a threat to religion of the spirit. The institution, with its orders and offices and privileges, must be kept inviolate. A leader, vested with authority and robed in the trappings of the church may violate the laws of his country which govern all his fellow-citizens; he may transgress the laws of God, deny the spirit of the religion he professes to minister, and live such a life as may be the way of death to the church and to the nation, yet he is unanswerable to anyone save the fellow-members of his own hierarchy. The life may not be scrutinized. Only the institution matters. Protect, defend, maintain the institution and its orders and privileges. Let the life be what it may. Ecclesiasticism is deaf to the word of Him who is the Head of the church, "Whosoever willeth to save his life shall lose it."

But it is not necessary to look across the ocean or into authoritarian churches to find evidences of ecclesiasticism. They may be heard in the pleas of politicians who pay lip service to the church and hope to ride into office upon their promises to "preserve our hallowed institutions." Their administration of office and the private conduct of their own lives may bear no resemblance to the standards of the religion they profess to champion. But the church has had a good word. Slogans of political groups make a fetish of the church and of religion. The life countenanced or encouraged by the office-holders may fester with graft, chicanery, prostitution, even lynchings. Still they seek support and election on the strength of their professed loyalty to the church. Office seekers inveigh against Communism because, say they, "It threatens our Christian institutions." They fail to perceive

131

that the real threat of Communism comes through the very failure of the Christians themselves to translate their religion into the highest ethic.

Even the church itself must be constantly on guard lest it become primarily concerned about the external outlines of its existence—numbers, wealth, power, organization, influence —and only secondarily occupied with the life which is the real fruit of the spirit. This revolutionary age has subjected the church to a fierce testing in many lands. Where the testing has been most withering one fact has stood out with condemning clearness. The church has been revealed as wholly intent upon building and maintaining an impregnable bulwark. It has been occupied chiefly with amassing treasure, accumulating wealth and power, and preserving its own life as an institution, and only incidentally concerned with the life of justice, righteousness, and true spirituality that finds its expression under the shadow of the institution. And where the future holds the possibility or the promise of revival, is where the forms and outlines of the institution have been smitten and the religion of the spirit is being recovered. It is where the leaders and people have ceased relying upon the temple or its current equivalent and have "hearkened unto the voice"—"Amend your ways and your doings."

Jeremiah's counsel to the captives in Babylon affords a striking insight into his essentially spiritual conception of true religion. His message was addressed to people who were desperately trying to recapture lost forms and institutions. "How can we sing the songs of Zion in a strange land?" They were sure that the breaking down of their nation meant the death of their religion. The songs of Zion needed all the surroundings of Jerusalem and its institutions if they were to be sung with any meaning or spirit.

The modern world has not entirely thrown off this conception of religious exercise and survival. The notion persists that religion is so involved with the forms, the institutions, the organization of society and the civilization in which it has flourished, that the destruction of any of these must be fatal to religion itself. The Church of England was once described as "the Tory party at prayer." That may have been a caricature of fact. But it does suggest a condition observable to all who will see that in many minds religion is identified with a form of society. Something dire will happen to religion if existing institutions, national organization, or civilization should be seriously disturbed—as though religion depended upon "civilization."

Jeremiah's advanced, untrammeled, and spiritual conception appears in this counsel to the captives.

Thus saith Jehovah of hosts, the God of Israel, unto all the captivity whom I have caused to be carried away captive from Jerusalem to Babylon: Build ye houses and dwell in them; and plant gardens and eat the fruit of them. Take ye wives and beget sons and daughters; and take wives for your sons, and give your daughters to husbands that they may bear sons and daughters and be not diminished. And seek the peace of the city whither I have caused you to be carried away captive, and *pray unto Jehovah for it*, for in the peace thereof shall ye have peace—For I know the thoughts that I think toward you, saith Jehovah, thoughts of peace and not evil to give you hope in your latter end. And ye shall call upon me, and ye shall go and pray unto me, and I will hearken unto you (29:4-12).

Like a stream from a hidden spring flows this counsel of the prophet. Deep within his soul is the reservoir of his knowledge of God. "God is spirit," One greater than Jeremiah was later to declare. That the prophet knew. He knew

133

that the true worship of God is a spiritual reality, dependent neither upon place nor ceremony. It cannot be identified with or confined to this nation and its institutions, and civilization, that the Hebrew people have so long considered God's alone. "Sing the Lord's song in a strange land, for is it not all the heavens and the earth that Jehovah fills?" True religion can be experienced and exercised "by the waters of Babylon" as truly as in Jerusalem. Jeremiah announces an eternal truth, which even a modern, enlightened age has not fully appropriated. The spiritual worship of God transcends all external forms, institutions, and organization. It will survive every assault and persist through all "change and decay."

LIFE AND THE CEREMONY

Jeremiah's energy was poured out in conflict not only against complacency that came of trust in the institution, but also against the ceremony that bore no fruit in life. Repeatedly the most penetrating and discerning of the Hebrew prophets had set in sharp contrast the ritual, and the life spirit and practice of their people. They had declared with unmistakable emphasis the demand of a spiritual religion for expression in a righteous, holy, and consistent life. Amos had challenged a people intent upon festival and ceremony with his forthright proclamation of religious duty, "I hate, I despise your feasts. I will take no delight in your solemn assemblies: yea, though ye offer me your burnt offerings and your meal offerings, I will not accept them. . . . Take thou away from me the music of thy viols. But let justice roll down as waters, and righteousness as a mighty stream" (Amos 5:21-24).

Isaiah, too, had protested in equally forceful language against the same spiritual deadness. "What unto me is the

134

multitude of your sacrifices?" saith Jehovah. "I have had enough of the burnt offerings of rams and the fat of beasts. . . . Wash you, make you clean, put away the evil of your doings from before mine eyes; cease to do evil, learn to do well; seek justice, relieve the oppressed, judge the fatherless, plead for the widow" (Isa. 1:11-17).

Jeremiah's voice was added powerfully and picturesquely to the calls of all the great prophets for a life that matched the liturgy.

To what purpose cometh there to me the frankincense of Sheba, and the sweet cane from a far country? Your burnt offerings are not acceptable nor your sacrifices pleasing unto me (6:20).

His was the same word that Samuel once spoke to a proud, victorious, but disobedient king: "To obey is better than sacrifice, and to hearken than the fat of rams" (I Sam. 15:22).

The temple sermon contained more than the prophet's protest against idolatry of the institution. From that central theme Jeremiah launched into an attack upon the evil that usually accompanies such a condition—idolatry of the ceremony.

Thus saith Jehovah of hosts, add your burnt offerings unto your sacrifices and eat ye flesh. For I spake not unto your fathers nor commanded them in the day that I brought them out of Egypt concerning burnt offering and sacrifices, but this thing I commanded them, saying, Hearken unto my voice and ye shall be my people; and walk ye in all the way that I command you, that it may be well with you (7:22, 23).

This speech contains implications that are really tremendous. Here the prophet actually makes the daring suggestion that the sacrifices and burnt offerings which were a part of the Hebrew system of worship were not originally ordained of God. This, in the eyes of his nation, amounted to blasphemy. He was questioning the divine ordinances. For the Hebrew people had come to believe that all the ceremonies pertaining to their ritual, all the ordinances of the temple system, the feasts and fasts, the burnt offerings and sacrifices, were directly given and appointed by God. There was efficacy in the performance of them. The nation was secure if the ritual was observed in its historic and traditional form.

The system of ceremonies and sacrifices had in fact developed from various sources. Many of its features, especially the sacrificial offerings, were to be traced to the rites and usages of other nations. Egypt, where the children of Israel were forged through suffering into a family, had contributed an important share. Originally these forms were designed to image forth certain truths of the religious relationship or to dramatize the act of worship. Conceivably they had value. But they finally came to be regarded as the worship itself, and few questioned the tradition of their divine origin. The ritual, to the mind of Jeremiah's day, had been constructed by God.

It was therefore nothing short of blasphemy to suggest that this whole system had any other origin than the direct commission of God to the fathers in the wilderness. Yet Jeremiah proclaimed it boldly in the very gate of the temple itself. "These forms that you so meticulously observe," he says, "these burnt offerings and sacrifices that you so scrupulously make, are not after all sacred. The real genius of your religion is not bound up with these things at all, nor is it expressed by them. The security of the nation is not dependent upon them. They are not of God. He did not command your fathers to keep this ritual. His word did not have to do with ceremonies but with life. What He said was, 'Hearken

136

unto my voice and ye shall be my people. Walk in the ways of my commandments that it may be well with you.'"

The intention of Jeremiah's soul and the nature of his conflict become very clear in the light of the historic reproductions of his situation. Jesus, face to face with a similar situation, poured out His spirit in both scorn and entreaty. "Go and learn what this means: I will have mercy and not sacrifice," was His word to a people whose spiritual dullness had obscured for them the ethical demands of true worship. "Woe unto you, scribes and hypocrites, ye cleanse the outside of the cup and the platter, but your inward parts are full of ravening wickedness," He said to men who worshiped the ritual but failed to see its relation to life. "You love to be seen in flowing garments, making long prayers, but it is only a pretense, for you devour widows' substance," was His piercing word to the smug devotees of the ceremony, who like the people of Jeremiah's day were "uncircumcised in their hearts."

Some of Jeremiah's ways of picturing the idolatry of the ritual are so vivid that they cannot fail to conjure up in the mind of the reader contemporary scenes. For example, the poem in the eleventh chapter is particularly expressive. A great gathering of the people in the temple apparently moved the prophet to protest against their blind trust in form and ceremony while they omitted the fundamental decencies of life. He poured forth his protest in a moving verse:

> What has My darling to do in My house?
> Vile are her doings!
> Can scraps of fat and sacred flesh
> Turn calamity from thee?
> Then mightest thou rejoice!
>
> —11:15; tr. by John Skinner

Reading this penetrating appraisal, one can see some modern congregation of comfortable, conventional, complacent people intent upon the observance of their ritual and satisfied with the correct performance of it. The rubrics are followed with meticulous care. The altar is properly dressed. All the appointments of the sanctuary are historically correct. Traditional usage is observed. Choir and liturgist are skilled in the techniques of worship, and offend in no particular. The worshipers are greatly edified. But they are apparently undisturbed by the blind spots in the life of which they are a part, that permit and even contribute to injustice, poverty, oppression, and moral delinquency. Irwin St. John Tucker in his "Meditations At Mass" in one sharp stroke sets up such a picture. He imagines a cynical smile coming over the Corpus Christi on His crucifix as the priest reads, "Feed my sheep," when just the day before a child in the neighborhood had died from what the doctors called malnutrition. Seated near the front of the church is a parishioner who has made his fortune from a corner on a food product. But he, too, listens complacently while white-robed choir boys sing "Inasmuch."

It was to precisely this sort of spiritual obtuseness that Jeremiah addressed his ringing challenge: "Can scraps of fat and sacred flesh turn calamity from thee?" "Ye people rend your hearts and not your garments" (Joel 2:12) was another prophet's way of summoning the congregation from ritual to reality. That same strange blindness to the moral requirements of a spiritual religion, to the emptiness of the form that touches only the circumference of the life, prompted Robert Herrick to pen his lines which repeat the prophet's challenge to every age:

138

Is this a fast—to keep
  The larder lean
    And clean
From fats of veal and sheep?

Is it to quit the dish
  Of flesh, yet still
    To fill
The platter high with fish?

Is it to fast an hour,
  Or ragg'd to go
    Or show
A downcast look and sour?

No, 'tis a fast to dole
  The sheaf of wheat
    And meat
Unto the hungry soul.

It is to fast from strife,
  From old debate
    And hate—
To circumcise thy life.

To show a *heart* grief-rent:
  To starve thy sin
    Not bin—
And that's to keep thy Lent.

—"A True Lent," ROBERT HERRICK (1591–1674)

"THE ETHIC OF JAHWE"

A translation by John Skinner of the phrase in 8:7, "the ethic of Jahwe" is at once illuminating and instructive. It reflects Jeremiah's understanding of both the source and the expression of the religious life. And it is a striking corrective of two widely encountered misconceptions concerning the nature of religion. On the one hand it answers the idea that religion is primarily a horizontal relationship and has as its all-consuming objective the realization of desirable ethical conditions. On the other hand, it corrects the notion that the religious life is a vertical relationship and consists entirely in the proper worship of God and the holding of correct beliefs about Him. Against both of these part-truths Jeremiah's speech here protests.

Yea, the stork in the heavens knoweth her appointed times; and the turtle dove and the swallow and the crane the time of their coming, but my people know not the *ethic of Jahwe* (8:7).

Unmistakably the prophet is pleading for the best life of society. But it is equally unmistakable that the life for which he pleads has its source in God. It is the "ethic of Jahwe." Jeremiah furnishes no aid and comfort to those eager reformers who suppose that the good life is achieved from without, who think of righteous living as a purely human exercise, and who start always at the circumference in their purpose to build a good society. Assemble the best-informed minds and the most socially inclined spirits, agree upon the blueprints, and summon the most skillful artisans: this is the proper procedure for the construction of the brave new world of justice, peace, and human brotherhood.

The humanist's thesis, "Man has within himself the powers and capacities requisite for the achievement of the good life," finds no echo in the preaching of Jeremiah. The program that begins with the effort to change the social order and omits the phases of worship receives no support from this reformer. "Prophetic preaching" is not, for this prophet at least, concerned first of all with the achievement of a certain kind of society, the accomplishment of certain reforms, and

140

the adoption of certain praiseworthy human relationships. For Jeremiah the good life begins with God. It is from his life of fellowship with God that he comes to throw himself unremittingly into the stern battle for the better world. For him the good life of society has its roots in the nature of God, and the relation of the worshiper to Him. This is the significant import of a poem of his early ministry in which he voices the lament of a God whose love has been sorely wounded.

> I remember the grace of thy youth,
> Thy love as a bride;
> How thou followedst me in the waste,
> In a land unknown.
> Holy was Israel unto Jahwe,
> First fruits of the harvest.
> —2:2, 3; tr. by John Skinner

"Holiness unto the Lord!" Here, for Jeremiah, is the reason, the deeper motivation, for the good life. No mere program of human excellence, no well-meaning list of moral resolutions, it is a life growing out of a vital union with God, as deep and actual as the life of the family.

If, however, the preaching of Jeremiah does not ignore the vertical relationship so often neglected by crusading preachers, neither does it ignore the horizontal. It is an overwhelming answer to all those critics who announce that religion is in reality evil because its primary concern is otherworldly, a long-range self-interest without any relevance to the life of the world that now is. Two conclusions are inescapable to the student of this prophet: The loss of God as Reality is fatal to the life of any people; and the true worship of God implies an ethic that is the expression of the moral character of God.

For Jeremiah this ethic was definite and positive. He was a protestant, constantly lifting his voice against specific evils that he saw in the life of his nation. But he was more. He was a protagonist, always contending for a life whose qualities were positive and clearly defined. No mere lamenter he, bewailing the prevalence of sins recognizable and deplorable. He had a strong apprehension of the kind of life that ought to characterize the nation worshiping the kind of God he knew. Two gross evils, untruthfulness and sexual profligacy, have been pointed out as the chief targets of his attack. In poem after poem and sermon after sermon, he did return to the assault upon these sins. But his preaching was never content with mere denunciation. It could not by any means be thought of in its logical impact as merely creating a vacuum in which men refrained from these sins or were satisfied if they should be dried up. Each of these vices was blacker because he saw it against the background of a life principle which he called "the ethic of Jahwe." For the positive realization of this kind of life he contended. In contrast with the sterility of a religion which had come to exhaust itself in the effort to preserve the institution and to observe the ceremony, the quality of life which he advocated had certain marked and positive characteristics.

Integrity in all human relationships was for Jeremiah the foundation of the "ethic of Jahwe." Possibly the most unhappy and disillusioning experience of his life was when he discovered that he could not trust the word or the oath of his fellow-men. Eugene Lyons, American newspaper correspondent and communist disciple, wrote a book, *Assignment in Utopia*, to describe his disillusionment as he came to Moscow expecting to find there the best fruits of the social reform he so ardently admired. Instead he found greed, sus-

142

picion, treachery, dishonesty, and oppression unmatched in the capitalist society from which he came. Jeremiah wrote a poem to describe a similar disappointment. His verse in Chapter 5 paints a vivid picture of a young reformer coming to Jerusalem expecting to find in that religious center all the finest fruits of the reform he had espoused, and discovering instead fraud and deceit, chicanery and dishonesty. With a tolerance not always manifested by him, he excused his first unhappy encounters, attributing them to the ignorance of the men he had happened to deal with. But soon he found that the condition was not limited to "the poor, the ignorant folk." All classes of society were infected. "The great ones," too, had burst all bonds and thrown off all restraints. He called upon the city to produce an honest person. Like Diogenes with his lantern, he sought through the streets and the market places for one man practicing the right and loving the truth. "Nay, when they say 'as Jahwe liveth' they swear to a lie." Not only was a man's word not as good as his bond. His bond was no good.

All of Jeremiah's remarkable genius for vivid expression was summoned to awaken his people to this failure of their life.

And they bend their tongue, as it were their bow, for falsehood; they are grown strong, but not for truth. . . . Take ye heed every one of his neighbor, and trust ye not in any brother, for every brother will utterly supplant, and every neighbor will go about with slanders. And they will deceive every one his neighbor and will not speak the truth. . . . Thy habitation is in the midst of deceit (9:3-6).

For among my people are found wicked men. They watch as fowlers lie in wait: they set a trap, they catch men. As a cage is full of birds, so are their houses full of deceit. Therefore are they became great, and waxed rich (5:26, 27).

For from the least unto the greatest every one is given unto covetousness . . . every one dealeth falsely (6:13).

The condition was shocking to the young prophet. It was shocking, not only because there was an evil that darkened the life, but because it existed against the background of God's faithfulness. It was a denial of the family relationship. Here is the significant feature of Jeremiah's preaching that must not be overlooked. His finger was always pointed to the integrity of God. This is the import of his appeals to nature: "The stork in the heavens knoweth her appointed times." "Dissolves from Sirion's crest the spotless snow?" All nature testifies to God's faithfulness. His smallest creatures bear witness to the integrity that is His. The deceit and the false-hood that have possessed the life of Judah cry out aloud because they are the denials of God in the life of man. And they carry the seeds of the nation's death.

Justice in the administration of all human affairs was for Jeremiah a further mark of "the ethic of Jahwe." The God he knew could not be worshiped truly in the midst of this mass of deceit and trickery. Men must be faithful to their agreements. But the ethic of Jeremiah's God implied something more. Not only must bargains be made and kept in good faith. The bargains themselves must be inherently just. A God who was known as justice and holiness could not be acceptably worshiped—however lavish the sacrifices and offerings—by men who administered their affairs with injustice. The worship of a just God must flower out into just living. Justice must flow down as waters and righteousness as a mighty stream.

144

The plainest and most practical example of this emphasis, which Jeremiah shared with all the great prophets, is to be seen in his insistence upon fair wages and the scorn with which he flayed unjust accumulation. The powerful, "the great ones," could use their power to multiply their wealth at the expense of underpaid laborers. There were men in Judah who closed their eyes selfishly to the rights of their fellow-men and supposed that the magnificence of their estates and the lavishness of their offerings could atone for failure to deal out justice in their human transactions. They waxed sleek and fat by the expedient of the unjust wage.

Against this brutal exploitation Jeremiah hurled every weapon in his armory. Sarcasm was his chief resort as he faced this evil. "As the partridge that sitteth on eggs she hath not laid, so is he that getteth riches and not by right" (17:11). He singled out the king for his most pointed assault. Aroused by Jehoiakim's gaudy and elaborate palace built virtually by unpaid labor, he moved to the attack.

Woe unto him that buildeth his house by unrighteousness and his chambers by injustice, that useth his neighbor's service without wages and giveth him not his hire, that saith, I will build me a wide house with spacious chambers, and cutteth him out windows, and it is ceiled with cedar and painted with vermilion. Shalt thou reign because thou strivest to excel in cedar? Did not thy father eat and drink, and do justice? Then it was well with him. He judged the cause of the poor and needy; then it was well. Was not this to know me? saith Jehovah (22:13-16).

A great preacher's great preaching is vocal and forceful in this speech. The pathway to the knowledge of God is declared to be the will to do God's will. Jeremiah appeals to the successful reign of Jehoiakim's father, Josiah, in the effort to open the eyes of the king who is blindly and stu-

145

pidly pursuing the road to destruction. Josiah knew God, not by any lavish impressiveness in the trappings of his rule, but by his devotion to the ways of God in all the administration of his office. Jehoiakim's devotion to sumptuousness, selfish indulgence, and lavish display not only wronged his neighbors at whose expense he profited, but closed the door effectually to the knowledge of God.

Jeremiah's stripping away the deceptive insincerity of externals to reveal the heart of true religion's fundamental demands paralleled the moral judgment of other great prophets. Micah set forth the same demand when he pictured the ineffectiveness and unacceptability of the most extravagant offerings, "thousands of rams, ten thousand rivers of oil"; and stated simply and directly the sum of human duty, "He hath showed thee, O man, what is good; and what doth Jehovah require of thee but to do justly and to love kindness, and to walk humbly with thy God?" (Mic. 6:7, 8).

The prophets here anticipate the principle which Jesus emphasized when He said, "If thou bring thy gift to the altar and there remember that thy brother hath aught against thee, leave there thy gift before the altar. Go thy way, first be reconciled unto thy brother, and then come and offer thy gift" (Matt. 5:23, 24). Nothing so effectively closes the pathway of man to God as the injustices that separate him from his fellow-man. No matter how large the gift, it is not acceptable to God if the worshiper owes an unpaid moral debt to his brother. The gift must wait before the altar until the ethic of God is made real in life.

Such a principle lays its solemn judgment upon many human transactions and much conventional worship. If God is not pleased with thousands of rams and ten thousand rivers of oil, apart from the worshiper's life of justice and love of mercy, no more is He pleased with millions of dollars in charities, philanthropies, and endowments if they come from a store accumulated by injustice. The silver and gold of the industrialist who establishes night schools for underprivileged children and lobbies against the enactment of child labor laws is more than slightly tarnished. The merchant who pays his salespeople minimum wages and out of the profits of his business endows a day nursery is condemned by the preaching of Jeremiah. The financial tycoon who contributes millions to his favorite philanthropy and grows rich by squeezing the thousands of small and trusting investors is in Jeremiah's speech "as the partridge that sitteth on eggs she has not laid." Francis G. Peabody, in one of his chapel talks to the students of Harvard University, said, "Many a man seeks to atone for hardness in making money by softness in distributing it. The test of religion in a man of business or any walk of life is not so much the way he gives his money as the way he makes it." Jeremiah was constantly applying that test. "Was not *this* to know *me?*" To do justice, to care for the cause of the poor and the needy, to find God and know Him in the humble following of His way and the practice of His will, was more acceptable than all sacrifices and burnt offerings, and was and ever will be the pathway into the deeper knowledge of God, which is life eternal.

Cleanness in sexual relations was yet another item in Jeremiah's understanding of the "ethic of Jahwe." The prophets made no effort to soften or tone down their language as they assailed the uncleanness of their people. Indeed, readers of Jeremiah may feel that he errs on the side of "plain speech" on this subject. Certainly there is no delicacy or reserve in his treatment of it. Several factors may account for this. The very prevalence of the evil was no doubt one element in

147

removing his restraint. What he saw in the life of the nation convinced him that the sickness called for extreme measures. His sometimes revolting language was the reflection of a revolting situation.

Furthermore, it is to be remembered that Jeremiah possessed a strong sense of the obligation of God's law. "Thou shalt not commit adultery" came to him with the sanction of God's own voice. He heard the thunders of Sinai in all the commandments of the Decalogue. They were reality to him. Their violation was rebellion against God. He saw the sin as black disobedience, and against that his religious concepts cried out.

But chiefly Jeremiah's emphasis and his extreme language may be traced to his perception of the importance of the family relationship. He thought of the nation's relation to God in terms of the family. The nation was like a bride unto God. Apostasy therefore was to him describable only as whoredom. It is to be recalled that no small part of Judah's sin was to be traced to the fleshly practices and associations of the pagan religions. The lustful nature of men combined with the seductive rites of the fertility cults to induce a life in which all restraints were thrown off. And Jeremiah's fine religious perception saw in all this a disgraceful infidelity to God, as well as an insidious force sapping the strength of the nation. The best life of the nation depended upon the strength and integrity of the family. And the family started with the relation to God.

It was the perception of this truth that made Judah's sin seem so stark and ugly to the prophet. He saw the crowds that assembled for the great national feasts or to celebrate some momentary victory. But whatever thrill he might have had at the sight of the multitudes gathered in the house of

God was deadened by his knowledge that the men of the nation "assembled themselves in troops at the harlots' houses" (5:7). When these people lifted their voices in the traditional psalms of their ritual, the prophet could only hear a confusion of sounds, for "every man neighed after his neighbor's wife" (5:8). When he looked at the altars he could have no religious feeling, for they suggested only harlotry, the faithlessness of the bride forsaking her husband, and the actual adulteries practiced beside the altars.

Modern nations in the aftermath of a global war may see very vividly the peril that alarmed the patriot Jeremiah. The urgencies of war lifted youths by the millions from a conventional life and settled them in great concentrations where the customs and restraints they had known and respected were removed. The immediate accompaniment of this new life was the increase of prostitution. Literally men "assembled themselves in droves at the prostitutes' houses." Sexual uncleanness became one of the commonplaces of the community's life. By many it was taken for granted. Venereal disease multiplied in its incidence. An important casualty of the war was the family. Divorces increased, with a still greater increase in prospect as the years pass. And the irony of it all, for those who see and care, is that the very measures designed to build the strength of the nation opened the way for the vice that will ultimately destroy that strength. The blameless damned, born and yet to be born, will carry for at least one generation the marks of the sexual profligacy induced by the madness of war.

The twentieth century sees this through the precise eye of the scientist. Jeremiah saw it with the no less understanding eye of the spiritual genius. He knew and worshiped a God who is seen most clearly by "the pure in heart." He thought of his nation as the family of God. He knew with deepest certainty that in the preservation of the family lay the strength and security of the nation. And he therefore pleaded in most extreme language for sexual cleanness as a mark of the "ethic of Jahwe."

An ideal society envisioned by the preaching of Jeremiah, but never realized in his day—when has it been realized?—would bear as its distinguishing marks these characteristics flowing from the worship of God. The world will never know whether the preaching of a man so unique, powerful, and consecrated as Jeremiah would have had salutary effectiveness had his ministry fallen earlier in the nation's history while there was yet hope for reclamation. But the world cannot fail to know the ideal for which he contended with all his energy and all his faculties.

The ideal society of Jeremiah's preaching would certainly leave unanswered many questions of social behavior which the twentieth-century mind raises. Problems of a religious man's attitude to such institutions as slavery, war, the profit motive, receive little or no illumination from his preaching. His indignation, poured out upon the treachery of the slave owners who freed the slaves when invasion threatened, only to repossess them when the threat receded (chap. 34), suggests the uneasy conscience of a religious man toward the whole institution that society accepts. Its implications certainly contributed to the only process that finally abolished the institution. But there was no clear ethic set forth in Jeremiah concerning this and other problems of social relationship which the passing years have made acute. No good purpose can be served by the effort to have the prophet speak upon a subject which had not achieved for him the stature of a social problem. Let the developing conscience and intelli-

150

gence of man, quickened by the religion of Jesus Christ, do that.

For Jeremiah the outlines of the "beloved community" were very simple, and equally clear. In his view the worship of God as an empty, unrelated form had no existence. An ethical life kindred in quality to the qualities he knew to be in God was for him the only evidence of reality in worship. A society of the true worshipers of the living God would be, in the preaching of Jeremiah, true, as God is true, just, as God is just, and pure in both heart and conduct, faithful members of God's family, as God is faithful to all His family upon earth. "Is not *this* to know me, saith the Lord?"

Jeremiah on the Nature and Consequences of Sin

TALKATIVE: "Where the grace of God is in the heart it causeth a great outcry against sin."

FAITHFUL: "Nay . . . I think you should rather say, It shows itself by inclining the soul to abhor its sin."

TALKATIVE: "Why, what difference is there between crying out against and abhorring of sin?"

FAITHFUL: "Oh! a great deal: A man may cry out against Sin of Policy but he cannot abhor it but by virtue of a godly antipathy against it. I have heard many cry out against sin in the Pulpit who yet can abide it well enough in the Heart, House, and Conversation."

—*Pilgrim's Progress*, JOHN BUNYAN.

Against the background of the professional religionists of his day whose every utterance was determined by "Policy," Jeremiah's hearty antipathy toward sin stands out in bold relief. Expediency has ever been the distinguishing mark of the ecclesiastical politician. Caiaphas settling the problem of Jesus: "It is expedient that one man should die," epitomizes the resort and reliance of his kind. Hilaire Belloc, interpreting the career of Woolsey, sympathetically, yet with the historian's concern for truth, has given to literature a clear

152

picture of the religionist who can "cry out against sin in the pulpit but who can yet abide it well enough in the heart, the home, and the conversation."

It would be difficult to place Jeremiah among these professional descriers of sin. There was that within him which "inclined his soul to abhor sin." The word of the Lord was, in his own vivid description, "a fire glowing in his breast, shut up in his bones, which could not be kept under." Out of this molten reservoir there poured forth a ceaseless stream, now of loving entreaty, now of solemn warning, and now of stern denunciation. And in this stream is to be clearly discerned the prophet's conception of the nature and consequences of sin.

At the start of Jeremiah's prophetic career it is quite evident that he conceived of the divine-human relationship primarily in terms of the nation. His earliest calls were summonses to national repentance. To Jeremiah sin was chiefly the sin of Judah. But his later emphases indicate that now he thinks of the nation as the collection of individuals. Its attitudes are the attitudes of the individuals who compose it. The sins of Judah are the sins of the *people* of Judah. The nation can turn to God only as men turn to God by the private decisions of their wills. As his insight deepens there runs through all his entreaties and warnings the appeal to the responsibility of the individual. Repentance and renewed life for the nation are dependent upon the choices of men, who, though they may be "lumped by their kind in mass, are singled by God unit by unit." As sin has been the choice of persons, so salvation must come through persons. It is in this emphasis that Jeremiah makes his most distinct and possibly most permanently significant contribution to the Old Testament's literature on the nature of sin. It was too long before the

153

formulation of a system of theology for the prophet to present any clearly defined doctrine of "total depravity" or "original sin." Yet he discloses insights and withal graphic descriptions that serve as perpetual guides to Christian thinking on this subject.

THE NATURE OF SIN

Jeremiah is no less aware of and concerned about actual sins than are others of the great prophets. He recognizes the specific defections of his people and calls them by name. When he denounces the sin of Judah it is not in general terms. He presents a bill of particulars, and his catalogue of the sins that flourish among his people is so definite that it could be duplicated by any square yard of the modern scene. The late Dr. Charles M. Jacobs, president of Mt. Airy Theological Seminary, speaking at the centennial celebration of Trinity Lutheran Church of Germantown, Pennsylvania, drew a striking picture of the changes that had taken place in the civic, social, industrial, and religious life during the hundred years of the congregation's existence. Then after a pause he said: "But there is one thing that has not changed. Sin has not changed since God gave Moses the Ten Commandments. I defy anyone to invent a new sin." Jeremiah's pictures of the life of his day are so sharp in their detail that he strongly justifies such a statement. He is aware of actual sins—the same sins that have plagued the life of man all through the centuries.

But he does not make the mistake of identifying these outbreaking acts with the sin itself which he knows is the real enemy of man. He looks elsewhere for his deepest definition. With sharp incisiveness he penetrates into the inner life and graphically describes the essentially spiritual quality of

154

sin. Following him through his succession of picturesque words and phrases, one feels that for Jeremiah sin may be summarized in its essence as *heart direction away from God.* Fundamentally he places sin, not in the outward act but in the heart condition. Not as a dispassionate observer and commentator on life, but as one who has held a mirror up to his own soul, and would describe that which he sees there, he sings his hymn of solemn confession:

> Deep beyond sounding is the heart
> And sick beyond cure
>
> Who can know it?
> —17:9; tr. by John Skinner

In a succession of pictures most vivid and striking, Jeremiah sets forth his concept of the inner nature of sin. The effect of his pictures is cumulative. If one asks this prophet, "What is sin?" the reply comes back, "Sin is crookedness"—

> Look at thy ways in the Valley
> And own thy deeds!
> A young camel light o' heel
> Zigzagging in her tracks.
> —2:23; tr. by George Adam Smith

The people once led in a straight path—pursuing a course marked out by God—have forsaken the way and are "zigzagging." Sin is misdirection. It is crookedness.

Sin is departure from integrity. A Roman poet singing of the ideal virtues of a good man struck his lyre on one clear note. *Integer vitae, scelerisque purus.*[1] First among the virtues fundamental to nobility of character always is integrity. Jeremiah finds the loss of this quality the real key to the

---

[1] Horace, Book I, Ode 22.

155

nation's failure. He is not the first, nor was he the last, of God's great spokesmen to find in communion with nature revelations of the character and intention of God. A poet of his people sang of "lifting his eyes unto the hills." From his home in Anathoth Jeremiah lifts his eyes to Mt. Lebanon and there reads the constancy of God in the never failing processes of nature. In contrast with the integrity of God revealed in nature he sees the deviousness of man. And he has one more abiding picture by which he drives home to the nation the quality of sin:

> Dissolves from Sirion's crest
> The spotless snow?
> Or cease the mountain streams
> Their ice-cold flow?
> But Me have my people forgotten
> They serve the unreal!
> Walking in paths uneven,
> A road unpaved.
> —18:14, 15; tr. by John Skinner

In a notable sermon preached to a broken, defeated German people, Dr. Hans Lillje exclaimed, "How often did I not feel the contrast between the wonderful world of God and the world of men." A noble spirit sensitive to the beautiful in nature moved with an invading force into one of the island paradises of the Pacific after days of heavy barrage had devastated it. One small corner of the island had escaped the general destruction. It stood, a spot of enchanting beauty in the midst of the wilderness produced by the wrath of man. This youth bowed his head in shame and prayed to God to forgive the sin of man against the handiwork of the Creator. So Jeremiah looks at the constancy of God written in the universe for all to read, and sees against the white snows of

Sirion the smudge of man's faithlessness as though to say, "Only man is vile."

Sin is "lifting the soul unto vanity." In the modern miracle of the radio there are in the receiving sets delicate filaments that stir and vibrate in response to the unseen impulses emanating from the station to which they are attuned. Like these filaments there is within man a faculty for response to that in life with which it is akin. The quality of man's soul is indicated by the nature of that to which he responds—"Deep calleth unto deep." A shallow nature lifts its soul unto vanity. A greedy spirit responds to the suggestion of profit. The fleshly nature is vividly alive to mammon. What a man is at the center of his being is revealed in the intuitive responses of his soul.

It is in this perception that Jeremiah's description of his people's sin is particularly revealing. "For my people are foolish, they know me not. They are wise to do evil. But to do good they have no knowledge" (4:22). "What hath my beloved to do in my house? Vile are her doings. . . . When thou doest evil thou rejoicest" (11:15). Possibly the most impressive picture of the state of soul of his people is that which Jeremiah gives us in the phrase which closes his scathing indictment recorded in the fifth chapter. "A wonderful and horrible thing has come to pass in the land. The prophets prophesy falsely, and the princes bear rule by their means and *my people love to have it so*" (5:30-32). So far from abhorring evil, so far even from practicing evil though hating it—"the sin that I would not, that I do"—the people actually *rejoice* in unrighteousness. They have "lifted their souls unto vanity." They "love to have it so." The filaments of the soul stir and respond, not to God, faith, spirituality, but to all in life which opposes His righteous rule.

157

Sin, in the speech of Jeremiah, is intractableness. He finds in the streets and bazaars of the cities one of his most illuminating pictures with which to confront his people with the essentially gross quality of their inner life. Another prophet has employed the same figure. "He shall sit," says Malachi, speaking of the ways of God, "as a refiner and purifier of silver" (Mal. 3:3). Many of the people whom the prophets addressed had seen the refiner of silver as he separated the precious metal from the dross with which in its original state it was combined. They had watched him as he subjected the molten mass to a fierce and yet fiercer heat. Only when he could see his own image reflected in the melted metal was he satisfied that the dross was all burned away and the purifying process complete. They had seen him reject a mass of the metal as his practiced eye perceived that, after the fire had done its utmost, what remained was lusterless dross. There was no valuable residuum of the desired silver. Of this process Jeremiah now reminds the people and paints into his picture of sin's reality one more telling stroke.

> An assayer I have set thee among My people
> To know and test their ways;
> They are wholly intractable stuff,
> Traders in slander—
> > Brass and iron all
> > Corrupt in life.
> The bellows snorts from the fire:
> > The lead is consumed!
> In vain does one smelt and smelt:
> > Their vileness will not out.
> Rejected silver men call them,
> > For Jahwe rejects them.

> —6:27-30; tr. by John Skinner

Crowning all these pictures stands Jeremiah's strongest word. Sin, he says, is stubbornness of heart. And the phrase by which he declares this is most significant. When he speaks of reformation and restoration, as in 3:15, 16, he pictures it as a people returning from the stubbornness of their ways and turning their *hearts* to God. "Neither shall they walk any more after the stubbornness of their evil hearts" (3:17). The apostasy of the nation is not merely a course of conduct. It is a way of life growing out of a willful spirit. "Because they have forsaken my law, and have not obeyed my voice, neither walked therein, but have walked after the stubbornness of their own hearts" (9:13, 14). "Behold ye walk every one after the stubbornness of his evil heart" (16:12). "We will walk every one after the stubbornness of his evil heart" (18:12). Eight times in the Book of Jeremiah the phrase recurs; but only twice in other portions of the Hebrew Bible, and then with a different meaning. Each time it is associated with the word "heart." The phrase is distinctively Jeremiah's. Its equivalent is variously: "the stubbornness of his evil heart,"[2] "the imagination of his evil heart,"[3] "induration of heart."[4] Repeated like a refrain by the prophet, this word adds a clear element to his definition of sin. Sin is in its essence the hardening of the heart against the overtures of God. At its root it is the proud assertion of self-will against the divine will, "induration of heart." But a mere word is not enough to describe the condition. Only a living figure that awakens the imagination will do. With superb imagery the prophet-poet sets forth this quality of sin in one unforgettable picture that must have spoken volumes to the people

[2] American Revision.
[3] 18:12; Driver.
[4] John Skinner.

of his own land. Sin is a powerful inner force as driving as the lust of a wild animal in the mating season.

> A heifer schooled to the desert
> In the heat of her lust,
> Snapping the wind in her passion,
> Who is to turn her?
> —2:24; tr. by George Adam Smith

Dante's *Divina Comedia* subtly but picturesquely presents this very truth about sin in the portrayal of the penitents' deliverance from purgatory. The poet pictures their recovery of paradise as the ascent of a steep mountain. At intervals along the mountain side are terraces at which successively the "seven deadly sins" are purged away. And Dante's true religious insight is discerned as he represents the first of these terraces to be that of pride. For pride is the primary sin. It is the very essence of sin. By it our first parents fell. And until it is completely burned away there can be no regaining of paradise. Milton—at the opposite pole of religious position —sees eye to eye with Dante in this. In *Paradise Lost* he answers the question of the cause of man's fall with the one word "pride."

> Who first seduced them to that foul revolt?
> The infernal Serpent: he it was whose guile,
> Stirred up with envy and revenge, deceived
> The mother of mankind, what time his pride
> Had cast him out from Heaven, with all his host
> Of rebel angels, by whose aid aspiring
> To set himself in glory above his peers,
> He trusted to have equaled the Most High.

Here, for these Christian thinkers, is the essence of sin. Here too for Jeremiah is the basic reality of sin, not in any

160

outward act, but in heart direction; in pride, willfulness, self-assertiveness. In the bold imagery of the prophet it is the young camel zigzagging in her tracks. It is the desert "heifer in the heat of her lust, snapping the wind in her passion."

The very forcefulness of Jeremiah's language permits no doubt about his understanding of the nature of sin. He seems to be drawing upon the full sweep of his poetic genius for words that will describe the truth he knows. He searches the whole realm of nature for living figures that will adequately portray the reality. He gives the impression that when he indicts the nation for specific sins, when he catalogues so accurately and vividly the actual vices that flourish among his people he is powerfully aware of an essential condition back of this body of conduct and productive of it. This is the fruit that has grown from the evil root. This is the stream that flows from the polluted spring. These are the manifestations of the disease within the life. They are the brood which —to paraphrase the word of St. James—"sin when it hath conceived brings forth."

Because Jeremiah is a sensitive soul and possesses the sharp imagery of a poet he perhaps excels others in his delineation of the actual transgressions of his people. His bill of particulars does not differ from that of others of the prophets. It does not differ from that of the moral analyst of any age. Indeed there are great passages in which he arraigns Judah and her leaders in language so contemporary that the reader has the feeling of listening to a man reporting tomorrow's headlines.

The sin of the heart conceives and brings forth sins of the hand and of the deed. What the brood is, is picturesquely described in passages already detailed in Jeremiah's report on the state of the nation—"This is the People." It is not neces-

161

sary here to repeat the prophet's description, but only to recall the roster. Sin when it has conceived, Jeremiah sees bringing forth adultery, brutishness, and lascivious living (5:7-9, 10:19-22, 13:27); untruthfulness, lying, and cheating (9:4, 5, 5:1, 2, 2:34); oppression (6:5, 6, 22:13-17); irreverence, profane and hypocritical usage (5:30, 23:1, 11); idolatry (10:1-10, 44:15-17).

"Fornicators, idolators, adulterers, covetous, drunkards, extortioners, and such were some of you" (I Cor. 6:9-11). The speaker is Paul, the time is the first century A.D., the place is Corinth. It could as well have been Jeremiah speaking in Jerusalem six centuries before Christ. A veritable horde of familiar sins troops across the pages of his prophecy. But always the reader is aware of the prophet's deeper perception and ascription of sin to the inner nature of man. Like a physician noting the pains and pallors of his patient that he may learn their hidden source, Jeremiah marks the procession of vices to see the disease behind them and proclaims his diagnosis, "Sick is the heart beyond cure." He sees the same condition which another has described in his language—"The whole head is sick and the whole heart faint."

The Consequences of Sin

As illuminating as are Jeremiah's insights concerning the nature of sin, his descriptions of sin's consequences are no less instructive. Manifestly the prophet's diagnosis of the moral and spiritual condition of Judah is not the result of a merely academic interest in the subject. He does not approach the question as one who would examine a speculative problem, satisfied if he can arrive at a correct definition. His concern has been awakened by what he sees sin doing and what it promises to do in the life of his people. This is his point of

162

impetus. The consequences of sin, clearly discernible in both their long and short term possibilities, set in motion the processes of his whole moral nature. Out of this come all the vivid pictures which tell the story of Jeremiah's concepts, and which contribute so pointedly to the religious thinking of all ages on this vital subject.

The enveloping, contaminating quality of sin is the first and most significant of the prophet's insights to impress the reader. He sees very clearly that sin does not stop with one sinner. It communicates itself to others. No man sinneth to himself alone.

Hast thou seen the backsliding Israel hath done? . . . And I said after she had done all these things she will return unto me; but she returned not. And her treacherous sister Judah saw it. And I saw when for this very cause backsliding Israel had committed adultery I had put her away and given her a bill of divorcement, yet treacherous Judah her sister feared not, but she also went and played the harlot. . . . And the whole land was polluted (3:7-9).

Because there is a solidarity of human society, any evil thing is certain to cross all the artificial boundaries that men create. Sin anywhere is like a disease that communicates itself and contaminates all life within its reach. Men are brothers whether they recognize the bond or not. When one brother is not safe, every other brother is imperiled. Thomas Carlyle relates an incident that strikes deeply into the social life of any period. An Irish widow in Edinburgh, destitute, went with her three children to seek assistance at the charitable establishments of the city. She was passed from one agency to another without being granted aid until, exhausted, she became a victim of typhus, died, and infected her lane with

163

fever, so that seventeen other persons died there. "Would it not have been economy to help this poor widow?" the narrator asked. "She took typhus fever and killed seventeen of you. Very curious! The forlorn Irish widow applies to her fellow-creatures as if saying, 'Behold I am sinking, bare of help; ye must help me! I am your sister, bone of your bone; one God made us.' They answer, 'No, impossible; thou art no sister of ours.' But she proves her sisterhood. Her typhus fever kills them; they actually were her brothers though they denied it."[5]

That which Jeremiah saw and declared so incisively has been the monotonous refrain of history. "Am I my brother's keeper?" say the sons of Cain seeking to deny the human bond. But the bond exists and ultimately forces recognition. To ignore it is impossible. To circumvent it is equally impossible. Sin cannot be contained. It has horizontal as well as vertical implications and involvements. A foul spot of evil practice appears on the face of the earth. It is in a remote and insignificant place. It concerns only a few unlettered, uncivilized people. Exploitation, injustice, oppression—the evil can be isolated and life may proceed comfortably in the favored, cultured centers. But inevitably at length the whole land is polluted. Like a pestilence the disease spreads and involves in its consequences innocent and guilty alike. The processes of history are inexorable.

Every age furnishes pointed instances of the truth. No more striking example exists than the world debacle of the twentieth century. A clever cartoonist, as the year 1945 drew to a close, summarized the uneasy state of the world by drawing a burned-out globe. Its gutted framework was surrounded

---

[5] Thomas Carlyle, *Past and Present*, Book III, *The Modern Worker*, Chap. II, "Gospel of Modernism."

by the mushrooming clouds of exploded atom bombs. On the vestiges of the North American Continent stood a charred skeleton like man, his bony hands clutching a telephone instrument. Into the transmitter he called, "Hello, hello, if there's any one left alive I'd like to unite with 'em in a world league to outlaw war." The end result forecast by that cartoon, not at all an impossibility, was one day represented by one or two limited conflagrations in isolated spots of great continents. Statesmen seriously proposed to limit them and their effects. Employing a different figure, the late President of the United States, Franklin D. Roosevelt, suggested this very possibility as he called upon the enlightened nations to "quarantine the aggressors." This policy, nobly conceived, expressed the revulsion of men of good will against the brutal indecencies of dictators drunk with the sight of power. It deserved to succeed. But against their will its adherents found themselves being drawn nearer to the catastrophe until they were a part of it and themselves finally the devisers, hurlers, and fear-stricken possessors of its most destructive weapon. It is impossible, life being constituted as it is, to block off a focus of evil, as foresters confine and control a blaze by cutting bare a wide path before the wind. Scientists may isolate a focus of physical disease but diseases of the soul cannot be isolated. Sin leaps the barrier. Hatred and aggression in Central Europe, exploitation and injustice on the rim of Asia or Africa, are not to be held in bounds by quarantine. No society or unit of society can surround itself with a "cordon sanitaire" and live in disregard of other units. Ultimately "the whole land is polluted."

Jeremiah furthermore sees the hardening quality of sin as one of its consequences and paints it with sharp, clear strokes into the pictures he draws.

> The sin of Judah is writ
> With pen of iron,
> With the point of a diamond graven
> On the plate of the heart (17:1).

This is his summary of the state Judah has reached after long years of resistance to God's varied appeals. It is a commentary on the state of his people rather than a dogma on depravity or repentance. The prophet is looking at a condition that at long last has come to pass. And he sees that condition the result of a cumulative process of hardening inherent in the nature of sin itself.

A superficial or fragmentary reading of Jeremiah's literature may suggest that he thinks of sin's punishment as a sort of *quid pro quo*. Man violates the law of God. God, to vindicate His justice, replies with a decree of punishment. "De Lawd" of *Green Pastures*, before the shadow of the God of Hosea was cast upon the scene, was characteristically leaning over the battlements of heaven impatient to hurl thunderbolts at His "sinnin'" subjects. Passages of Jeremiah's writings might be cited to support such an idea of God; or the kind of deity that H. G. Wells describes in his *God the Invisible King* under the title, "God and the Nursery Maid." He says: "For many of us the word God first came into our lives to denote a wanton and irrational restraint, as Bogey, as the All Seing and quite ungenerous Eye. . . . I thought of Him as a fantastic monster, perpetually spying, perpetually listening, perpetually waiting to condemn and strike me dead."[6]

But only a fragmentary reading of the prophet can support such a thought of God. This would be to ignore both

---

[6] H. G. Wells, *God the Invisible King* (Lond.: The Macmillan Co., 1917) pp. 43 f.

the total import of his message and the poetic quality of his speech. When he calls upon all his soaring power to declare the "wrath of God against sin"—"shall I not visit for these things?"—he is not prosaically announcing the arbitrary decree of an offended deity. He is describing the operation of an inherent force. He is proclaiming the inevitable consequence of sin. Sin hardens, not because a wrathful God has imposed the exact penalty His justice demands, but because this is its nature and quality.

Jeremiah sees the punishment of sin taking two forms. Sin hardens. "Your sin"—after long, heedless years—"is writ with a point of iron." "And Jehovah said unto me: Pray not for this people for their good. When they fast I will not hear their cry; and when they offer burnt offering and meal offering I will not accept them" (14:10-12).

Jeremiah sees the sin of his people, long nurtured and practiced, hardening, ever hardening. Like the path beaten into the soil by the passing of many feet, the soul of this people has become impervious to the softening influence of God's word. And the prophet, yielding to despair, strikes this minor key in his song of hopelessness:

> Can the Ethiop change his skin,
>   Or the leopard his spots?
> Then also may ye do good
>   Who are wont to do evil (13:23).

Sin is destructive. Most pronounced in the total picture of Jeremiah's message is this stroke. Sin's chief punishment is the sin itself, and the destruction its self-multiplication accomplishes. "Be thy scourge thine own sin" (2:19). Frederick G. Banting, seeking to discover the cause and nature of one of man's most distressing maladies, diabetes, relied upon the operation of a certain law in the physical world. Earlier scientists had by their researches pointed to the pancreatic glands as the seat of the human system's failure to convert sugar into heat and energy. But just what portions of these glands were guilty? To ascertain this Dr. Banting tied off various sections of the glands of animals so that they were prevented from functioning. He relied upon the law in physical nature that the organ thus prevented from performing its function would atrophy. And proceeding thus he discovered the relation to the disease of a substance in these glands, known as the Islands of Langerhans. One of the triumphs of modern scientific research was achieved because a scientist could depend upon the law: a faculty misused or unused dies.

In the same sense "the soul that sinneth dies." "The wages of sin is death" not because a celestial paymaster has calculated to a nicety the penalty for a bargain not kept, but because the order of created life operates.

This truth is written into Jeremiah's total disclosure of the consequences of sin.

Thus saith Jehovah, the God of Israel, Every bottle shall be filled with wine; and they shall say unto thee, Do we not certainly know that every bottle shall be filled with wine? Then shalt thou say unto them, Thus saith Jehovah: Behold, I will fill all the inhabitants of this land, even the kings that sit upon David's throne and the priests and the prophets and all the inhabitants, with drunkenness. And I will dash them one against the other. I will not pity, nor spare, nor have compassion (13:12-14).

The punishment of the drunkard is that he shall be filled with drunkenness. The consequence of sin is more sin, a bestial self-destroying fullness of sin!

When the Japanese beetle infestation was at its height in the New Jersey and Pennsylvania area, where it originated in the United States, the greenskeeper of a country club hazarded a prediction concerning its course, a prediction fulfilled by events. An observer, distressed by the destructiveness of the insects and their rapidly multiplying numbers, asked how they could be prevented from destroying all the grass and foliage in that area. The greenskeeper replied: "The history of these pests is that the colony becomes so strong that it destroys itself. Its numbers accumulate until the accumulation creates a disease like foul brood which finally leaves only a weak remnant."

The concentrations of wealth and power in the colonies of human civilizations, too, are subject to the decay that comes from too great accumulation. Moth and rust do consume. The law of diminishing returns follows swiftly upon the heels of the law of increasing returns.

A pointed example of the practical operation of this principle impressed itself upon an observer of the life of a large industrial city of America. In the early 1920's this city had in an obscure corner a particularly shameful slum area. Huts improvised from packing boxes were huddled in a ravine over which crossed a bridge to one of the city's finer residential sections. Windows and doors in these hovels were openings at which burlap provided the only protection against the elements. Women performed their backbreaking daily chores in the midst of indescribable squalor. Children were spawned to grow up—if they survived—in dust and mire. The community was as depressed in all its aspects as it was sunken in its location.

Looking from one rim of the ravine across to the other, the observer could see, if he did not allow his gaze to drop downward, the gardens and homes of the moderately wealthy. He could turn a few blocks in another direction, almost within sight of the ravine slum, and find himself in a street lined on either side with the palaces of the city's multimillionaires. The most impressive show places of the community were there, great cut-stone mansions, surrounded by luxurious lawns, adorned with handsome shrubbery. It was unbelievable that such a juxtaposition of sumptuous, showy wealth and abject poverty could exist. It awakened disquieting thoughts. Even as the mansions impressed the observer with the security and strength of the industrial civilization of the era, the sunken slums demanded an answer.

Twenty years later the observer revisited the city of contrasts, and this phenomenon impressed him: The city's street of once-magnificent dwellings had become a veritable waste. One mansion after another had been torn down. Rubble marked the location of former palaces. Brambles grew where hybrid rhododendron had flourished. Crumbling terraces were reminders of costly landscaping projects. Here and there a vegetable garden relieved the scene of desolation. But for miles the street, once the site of the city's best tax resources, traversed a dreary waste awaiting humbler rehabilitation. The years had exacted their pay. To the credit of the city it was noted that the mean street of slums, too, had disappeared. But somewhere in the eternal processes of life the inexorable laws had operated. Accumulation had become so great that it consumed itself. The very concentration of wealth had created conditions that made the mansions untenable and dictated their destruction. The moth and rust of modern life had consumed.

One prophetic voice after another warned the Hebrew people of this very peril to their life. Hosea, in keeping with

the style of his prophecy, pictured it in terms of the barren-
ness resultant from harlotry. The abuse of nature's gift of
fruitfulness results in the loss of the capacity to bear fruit.
"Give them, O Jehovah—what wilt thou give? give them a
miscarrying womb and dry breasts. . . . Ephraim is smitten,
their root is dried up, they shall bear no fruit (Hos. 9:14, 16).
Amos saw in the very wealth and luxury of Israel's palaces
the portent of their destruction: "The adversary shall bring
down thy strength, and thy palaces shall be plundered. . . .
I will smite the winter house with the summer house; and
the houses of ivory shall perish and the great houses shall
have an end" (Amos 3:11, 15). Habakkuk resolved the
doubts that beset him as he pondered the vaunting triumph
of evil forces by mounting to his high tower and there seeing
things in their true perspective. One of the truths that became
apparent to him from that vantage point was the self-destruc-
tiveness of evil. Overweening accumulation, like the multiplying brood, destroys itself. "Woe to him that getteth an
evil gain for his house, that he may set his nest on high . . .
Thou hast devised shame to thy house by cutting off many
people and hast *sinned against thy soul.*" (It is noteworthy
that the prophet sees the extortioning landlord not merely
sinning against his oppressed tenant, but "sinning against
his own soul.") "For the stone shall cry out of the wall, and
the beam out of the timber shall answer it" (Hab. 2:9-11).
The house built by greed and oppression carries within
itself the elements of its own downfall. Its very timbers and
masonry protest aloud. "The stars in their courses fight
against Sisera."

For Jeremiah this truth exists in the figure of the woman
of pleasure. She has given herself to her lovers until she can
no longer make herself attractive. Her very self-abandon-

ment has destroyed her capacity to attract. The ones upon whom she has bestowed her favors despise her.

And thou, when thou art made desolate, what wilt thou do? Though thou clothest thyself with scarlet, though thou deckest thyself with ornaments of gold, though thou enlargest thine eyes with paint, in vain dost thou make thyself fair. Thy lovers despise thee (4:30).

As Jeremiah contemplates the decay which Judah's stubborn devotion to her idols of sin has wrought within her, he mourns above all else the loss of character. From what heights has she fallen! The shame of her low estate is silhouetted against the noble creation she might have been. And this complete corruption of nature is made the theme of the prophet's lament (2:21):

> Yet a noble vine did I plant thee,
>   Wholly true seed;
> How couldst thou change to a corrupt,
>   A wildling grape?

THE RESPONSIBILITY FOR SIN

To those who argue that man is caught in the grip of forces over which he has no control and which hasten him on to an unwanted destiny Jeremiah has an answer. In his day the refusal to accept personal responsibility took the form of quoting a proverb which had become something of a cliché. "The fathers have eaten sour grapes and the children's teeth are set on edge." Men seized upon what is unquestionably one of the most tremendous facts of life, the fact of heredity, and thrust it forward to blunt the demand for accountability in the area of the moral and social life. They looked at their evil state and perhaps deplored it. "But," said

172

they, "after all we are not the ones responsible. We are reaping the harvest of our fathers' sowing. We are the playthings of fortune. Powerful forces have been at work, long before our day, shaping, molding, directing, until today we are the prisoners of blind elements of time. The fathers have eaten sour grapes."

One can almost hear a modern voice repeating, "Man is only a midge infesting the epidermis of one of the lesser planets." Or one can hear another voice declaring,

That Man is the product of causes which had no prevision of the end they were achieving; that his origin, his growth, his hopes and fears, his loves and his beliefs are but the outcome of accidental collocation of atoms; that no fire, no heroism, no intensity of thought or feeling, can preserve an individual beyond the grave; that all the labors of the ages, all the devotion, all the inspiration, all the noonday brightness of human genius are destined to extinction in the vast death of the solar system, and that the whole temple of man's achievement must inevitably be buried beneath the debris of a universe in ruins—all these things if not quite beyond dispute are yet so nearly certain that no philosophy that rejects them can hope to stand. Only within the scaffolding of these truths, only on the foundation of unyielding despair, can the soul's habitation henceforth be safely built.

Brief and powerless is Man's life; on him and all his race the slow, sure doom falls pitiless and dark. Blind to good and evil, reckless of destruction, omnipotent matter rolls on its relentless way.[7]

Moral accountability in this kind of universe? "The fathers did eat sour grapes and the children's teeth were set on edge."

The first recorded divine-human encounter involved this

---

[7] Bertrand Russell, "A Free Man's Worship," in *Mysticism and Logic* (New York: W. W. Norton & Co., Inc., 1929) pp. 47 f., 56.

principle. God "walking in the garden in the cool of the day" confronted man, His child made in His own image. The man had employed the capacities inherent in this endowment for willful self-assertion against the divine will. And this man, hiding from God, yet unable to hide, answered the divine pursuer with an instinctive resort to the plea of nonresponsibility. "The woman thou gavest to be with me, she gave me of that fruit of the tree and I did eat." The one who has failed is not responsible for the failure. A creator who has surrounded him with the elements of his environment is responsible. Man is the product of the forces that touch his life. But the voice of God smote with all its implications the ear of evading man: "Adam, where art THOU?"

Like that insistent demand of God, whose messenger he knew himself to be, is Jeremiah's word to Judah. Paradoxically, he finds almost his only message of hope in the darkest days of Jerusalem's first captivity. What one scholar (George Adam Smith) calls "The Release of Hope" comes to him when the blow has fallen. Then as the purifying processes of affliction begin to operate Jeremiah sees a new and spiritually strengthened Jerusalem arising out of the ruins of the old. He sees these people, refined as through adversity, no longer seeking refuge in the old cliché. They accept the responsibility which belongs to a child of God endowed with the qualities that constitute the image of God in man. And for all ages to come the prophet proclaims the religion of personal responsibility—the dignity, the worth, and the accountability of the individual.

In those days they shall say no more, The fathers have eaten sour grapes and the children's teeth are set on edge. But everyone shall die for his own iniquity: every man that eateth sour grapes, his teeth shall be set on edge (31:29, 30).

174

Centuries later another poet facing a devastating personal experience found final comfort and assurance in the knowledge of a deep Christian experience. Sorrow, and the doubts induced by sorrow, had been his portion. But in the Christian relationship he found that which brought an abiding peace. The truth vocal in his hymn of dedication is the truth of Jeremiah baptized into the name of Christ.

> Strong Son of God, Immortal Love,
> Whom we, that have not seen Thy face,
> By faith, and faith alone, embrace,
> Believing where we cannot prove;
>
> Thou seemest human and divine,
> The highest, holiest manhood Thou;
> Our wills are ours, we know not how;
> Our wills are ours, to make them Thine.
>
> —"In Memoriam," ALFRED, LORD TENNYSON

Jeremiah and "The Tragic Sense of Life"[1]

Tragedy blazed into the Empire State building in New York City upon a foggy Saturday morning in the summer of 1945. A low-flying army plane, its pilot blinded by the fog, crashed into one of the upper stories of that towering edifice. The resultant shock and ensuing explosions spread panic and death of a peculiarly horrible nature. When this flaming death thrust its shape into that honeycomb of offices it chose, by a strange irony, to enter the suite occupied by a charity organization of the Roman Catholic Church. There must have been many offices in the building leased by agencies and corporations of a wholly secular character and intent only upon material profits. But this disaster passed by them all and singled out the space occupied by the benevolent arm of a Christian church, choosing to inflict suffering and death upon the agents of mercy. As the news of the tragedy swiftly spread throughout the nation, it wrung from millions of lips the inevitable question: "Why?" It seemed to pinpoint the age-old, universal perplexity of man. How can a man relate himself to the tragedy and especially the unmerited sufferings which thrust themselves upon his consciousness on every hand? If, as the Christians profess to believe, the universe is

---

[1] The title is derived from the work of Don Miguel Unamuno.

176

presided over by a just and loving God who is all-powerful and by whose eye the fall of the sparrow is marked, why do tragedies like that of the Empire State building occur?

It is precisely upon the rock of this perplexity that the faith of multitudes comes to shipwreck. Youths sleeping peacefully in a dormitory at Dartmouth College are quietly overcome by escaping fumes of coal gas, and many homes, including that of a Lutheran pastor visited by double tragedy, are plunged into darkest grief. School children in Texas, engaged in the educational pursuits required of them by their state, are suddenly blown by a terrific explosion against the walls of their schoolrooms, and a pall of sorrow settles over a community bereft of its fair children. Economic dislocation wipes out the fruits of past labor and thrift and destroys present opportunity and future security, and a whole society faces the specter of fear as human morale crumbles. Worldwide warfare sweeps down upon the nations, claiming the finest of the youth, breeding misery, fear, destruction, and sorrow, and unloosing the "Four Horsemen of The Apocalypse" to ride devastatingly throughout the earth. And as "the tragic sense of life" possesses our minds and spirits we lift from broken hearts and trembling lips the question, "O God—if there is a God—why?"

Modern man does not need clever and sophisticated writers to stir him up to an awareness of his problem. His own experience confronts him inescapably with it. But current literature has a way of focusing the thoughts of men upon it and making it articulate. Thus Oscar Wilde declares bluntly the disquieting thought that has been awakened in many minds when he says, "There is enough suffering in one mean London street to prove that there is no God." Anatole France exclaims, "Man has been called the lord of creation.

He is the lord of suffering." And H. L. Mencken summarizes the common human dilemma when he reserves for the last paragraph of *Treatise on the Gods* a list of the unconquered diseases that inflict their torture upon men, and there leaves the subject with the subtle question his description raises unanswered.

That question was flung out on the first atheist radio broadcast. Robert H. Scott, arguing the case for atheism, predicted that seventeen million people now living will die of cancer. "Do not speak to me," he added, "of an almighty God who is merciful and just!"

The perplexity with its hazard for faith is as old as human thought. It wrote the Book of Job, that ancient drama which revolves about the problem of unmerited suffering and is introduced, significantly enough, by Satan's sneer, "Doth Job serve God for nought?" It wrung from a psalmist's lips the exclamation which phrases the very thought of universal mankind, "My feet were well-nigh slipping when I saw the prosperity of the wicked" (Ps. 73:2). It called forth the skeptic's question upon which the Book of Habakkuk hinges, "If there is a God, why does He not act in history?" It cast at Jesus the question, "Who did sin, this man or his parents, that he was born blind?" And it drew from Him the words, "Think you that those upon whom the tower of Siloam fell were guilty above others?" with its implication that there is no glib, easy explanation for suffering, and the spirit of man must reckon with the reality.

TRAGEDY AND THE EVERLASTING "WHY?"

So much of our common humanity appears in Jeremiah that we should not be surprised to find this problem vocal throughout his work. The situation he faced, as well as the

178

experiences he met, was calculated to make the "tragic sense of life" particularly vivid to him. He saw with unerring vision the fate that awaited his own nation, the people who for generations had been taught that they were the special objects of God's care. Habakkuk has a particularly pungent passage in which he describes the ruthless fury of the invading Chaldeans: "Thou that art of purer eyes than to behold evil and that canst not look on perverseness, wherefore lookest thou on them that deal treacherously and holdest thy peace when the wicked swalloweth up the man that is more righteous than he: and makest men as the fishes of the sea, as the creeping things that have no ruler over them?" (Hab. 1:13, 14). This very invasion Jeremiah foresaw and experienced. The people of Norway, after the first World War, hospitably sheltered, fed, and nurtured the children of defeated Germany. When the fury of the Wehrmacht struck out in 1940 one of the first acts was the seizure of Norway by specially trained troops led by these very youths whose lives had been preserved and their strength nourished in the Christian homes of the invaded land. Like some Norwegian patriot seeing fanatical Nazi youths installed by force as the rulers of his cities and villages, and crying out of his helplessness for justice, Jeremiah saw the invading hordes of the Chaldeans "swallowing up the people more righteous than they," and he lifted his searching cry for judgment.

Moreover his own personal experiences were likely to make him poignantly aware of the problem. Jeremiah's was no mild passive nature. His natural disposition was rebellious and vindictive. His sense of fair play and justice was markedly developed. He was not the kind of person to acquiesce in every wrong inflicted upon him, to "take it" with a gesture of resignation. The fifty-third chapter of Isaiah fits, in many of its descriptions, the experience of Jeremiah. But these words in it do not describe him: "as a sheep before its shearers is dumb, so he opened not his mouth." To flare up, to strike back, to rebel openly was his typical reaction. When, therefore, suffering became his lot in consequence of his advocacy of what he knew so certainly, and felt so strongly was right, he could not be silent. Because the truth he preached was so clearly perceived as the word of the Lord, because the sin he denounced was so patently the defiance of God, everyone who opposed him became to him the enemy of God. Few men in history have been compelled to suffer indignity, hostility, and personal cruelty so undeservedly or so pointedly because of the failures of others, as was Jeremiah. Given his turbulent, justice-loving nature and the persecutions that became his lot, the "everlasting why" is an inevitable outcome.

Thus this perplexed soul asks the question that men have ever asked in the midst of life's bitter experiences. And his wording of it could find an echo in the speech of any bewildered person today.

Too righteous art thou, O Lord, that with thee I should argue; yet causes there are I must speak to thee of: the way of the wicked—why doth it prosper, and the treacherous all be at ease? Thou hast planted them, they all take root, they get on, yea, they make fruit. Near in their mouths art thou, but far from their hearts (12:1, 2).

Puzzled by the events of history and the difficulty of interpreting them in the light of all his people have believed about the providence of God, this prophet exclaims:

Then I said, Ah, Lord God! Thou hast deceived this people,

180

saying, "Ye shall have peace"; and now the sword has pierced to the life (4:10; tr. by John Skinner).

In one of the passages in which he sets forth confidently the retributive action of God toward a faithless people, Jeremiah incidentally voices the common question of mankind. As he pictures the destruction that shall overtake Jerusalem, he asks the question, "Why hath Jehovah done thus to this great city?" (22:8). While this is a rhetorical question designed to launch the prophet's declaration of God's visitation of punishment upon a rebellious people, there is yet apparent the underlying assumption that men intuitively fling such a question at God when tragedy approaches, "Why hath the Lord done this?"

Marking his rebellion as the men of Anathoth seek his life, his sulking as his early prophecies seem unfulfilled, his bitter ignominy as he sinks into the mire of the cistern, and listening to the voice of his perplexity as he stubbornly asks his questions of God, the reader of Jeremiah feels that here is the tortured mind of "Everyman" expressing itself in the insistent challenge to religious faith—"Why?"

The problem of the presence of tragedy in a world in which God rules is articulate in the Book of Jeremiah. No modern writer states it more forcefully. For it the prophet has his own answer. His answer is not so complete and satisfying as that supplied by a total Christian revelation, yet it has relevance and value. There are really three avenues into which Jeremiah's literature leads, each contributing something important to the thinking of religion on this subject. One is his simple, direct answer for the problem, possibly an oversimplification. Another is his indirect answer. And the third is a deductive answer, a road to which his own use of his experience points the way. And possibly this is the most important and revealing of all.

TRAGEDY AS DIVINE VISITATION

Like many of the prophets of his day, Jeremiah saw in the calamities and evil that came upon Judah the direct visitation of God. The suffering that the nation endured, even the catastrophes of nature as well as the greater misfortunes yet to come, were to him, in some measure, the operation of the hand of God. They were moreover the plain, direct punishments of God, His reply to the sins of His people. Jeremiah was not unique in this, either in his own day or since. Prophets before him had declared it with unmistakable emphasis. And this conception of the origin of tragedy has again and again been repeated. Job's accusers reappear with every tragic circumstance of life to say, "Remember, I pray thee, who ever perished being innocent? Or where were the upright cut off? According as I have seen, they that plow iniquity and sow trouble reap the same. By the breath of God they perish. And by the blast of his anger they are consumed" (Job 4:7-9).

Jeremiah possibly stated this view with greater naiveté than did others of God's spokesmen. The eternal "therefore" rings out repeatedly in his message: *"Therefore* have the showers been withheld" (3:3). *"Wherefore* I will make my words in thy mouth a fire" (5:14). *"Therefore* I am full of the wrath of Jehovah" (6:11). *"Therefore* saith Jehovah, behold I will lay stumbling-blocks before this people" (6:21). *"Therefore* pray not for this people for I will not hear thee" (7:16). *"Wherefore* the land is perished and burned up like a wilderness" (9:12). "Thou hast rejected me, saith Jehovah,

182

thou art gone backward, *therefore* I have stretched out my hand against thee" (15:6).

Like a refrain the word is repeated. Jeremiah saw, to his own conviction, the relation between the sins of the people and the disasters that came upon them. And to a large degree he interpreted this as the direct action of God. Suffering came because men angered God with their sins. The drought (chap. 14) is represented thus as a direct visitation of God. The vivid picture drawn by the prophet suggests in many of its features that with which men have frequently become familiar—empty cisterns, cattle deserting their young, fields blackened, animals panting, the people praying for relief. Sections of the United States experienced or witnessed scenes just like this in 1930 and the following summer. Jeremiah's explanation of it is precisely what was often heard in the stricken areas of this country:

Thus saith Jehovah, Even so have they loved to wander; they have not refrained their feet, *therefore* Jehovah doth not now accept them. Now will he remember their iniquity and visit their sins. . . . Pray not for this people for their good. When they fast I will not hear their cry; and when they offer burnt offering and meal offering I will not accept them, but will consume them by the sword, and by the famine and by the pestilence (14:10-12).

The classic description (chap. 5) of a faithless, unruly, wicked people is intertwined with a description of the wrath of God against sin.

Shall I not visit for these things? saith Jehovah; and shall not my soul be avenged on such a nation as this? . . . And it shall come to pass when ye shall say, Wherefore hath Jehovah done these things unto us? Then shalt thou say unto them, Like as ye have forsaken me and served foreign gods in your land, so shall ye serve strangers in a land not your own (5:9, 19).

One of the clearest declarations of this concept is the description, already referred to, of Jerusalem's disaster.

And many nations shall pass by this city and they shall say every man to his neighbor, Wherefore hath Jehovah done this to this great city? Then shall they answer, Because they forsook the covenant of Jehovah their God and worshiped other gods and served them (22:8, 9).

Thus Jeremiah regards the evil that has come to Judah as the direct visitation of God. The nation suffers because it has sinned.

Thou hast rejected me, therefore have I stretched out my hand against thee. This people hath a revolting and rebellious heart. . . . Neither say they in their heart, let us now fear Jehovah our God that giveth the rain, both the former and the latter in its season: that preserveth unto us the appointed weeks of the harvest. Your iniquities have turned these things away and your sins have withholden good from you (5:23-25).

There can be no question but that Jeremiah sees in the calamities of the people the hand of God stretched forth in retribution.

This at once awakens certain queries. Is this an adequate conception of God? Does Jeremiah have a God worthy of man's devotion? How far, for example, are men justified today in such an explanation of evil? Can we say that the scourge of a global war is the punishment of God sent upon a sinful world? Do we not in such an explanation raise more questions than we propose to answer? One can see some of these questions striking at the very character of God. What

184

kind of God is this who inflicts suffering upon innocent and guilty alike?

Regardless of the difficulties this fact raises, it must be said that the God of Jeremiah is a God who visits with stern punishment His people who transgress His laws and forsake His ways. This is the God the prophet knows. This is his explanation of at least some of the tragedy of life. But having said this, one is bound to point out also certain qualifying truths. One of these truths is that the prophet's emphasis, the frequence and vehemence of his declarations of tragedy as the punitive activity of God, grows to some degree out of the extremity of the situation he faces. An earlier prophet, speaking while there was yet large hope of recovery and restoration, could well magnify the mercy of God and strike more frequently the pleading note. But Jeremiah is addressing a nation all but "in extremis." He sees a people wholly rebellious, facing total disaster, and in the very nature of the case he must apply every measure to awaken, convince, and turn them. The advanced stage of their deterioration calls for severe speech and extreme measures.

A second qualifying factor is an appreciation of the "how" of Jeremiah's understanding of God's visitations. Although he regards the calamities of the nation as the visitation of God, he does not in any sense think of this God as a merely vengeful Deity who rejoices in the vindication of His majesty through the discomfiture of His people. Plainly Jeremiah sees the punishment as an integral part of the moral quality of God. It is the inevitable consequence of sin. The prophet's thought in all this is bound up with his idea of the covenant. A covenant to the Hebrew mind, and indeed in its essence, involved not merely the obligation to bless the people who kept their covenant, but also the obligation to

185

punish those who broke it. The covenant of God could be broken on His part as well by failure to punish as by failure to bless. The very righteousness of God was at stake. "Ye shall be my people and I will be your God" (30:22). Jahwe could not be their God if they persistently and stubbornly rejected all His overtures and refused to be His people. This truth was for Jeremiah of paramount importance. However reluctant God might be to punish, His impulse to withhold punishment was estopped by the willfulness of His people. The covenant must not be broken in either of its equations. He could not act otherwise in view of His own righteousness and the terms of His covenant. "How else can I do?" is the prophet's way of declaring the moral necessity. God is bound by His own moral character.

Furthermore, those who mark the emphases of Jeremiah and see in them only the description of a stern, justice-dealing Deity miss a note that rings out repeatedly in the prophet's message. The note of pleading, though never dominant, is never quite silenced by the overtones of Sinai's thunders. Even his "How else can I do?" seems to be spoken with a break in the voice. The God of Jeremiah, seen not merely in one mood of the prophet's speech, but in his entire conception, suffers with his people. He addresses them at times with the yearning speech of wounded love. He agonizes because they suffer for their transgressions.

Abraham Lincoln's second inaugural closes with a speech which is a faint human picture of the truth that appears to discerning eyes in the deeper reaches of Jeremiah's pleading. "The Almighty has His own purposes. 'Woe unto the world because of offenses, for it must needs be that offenses come; but woe to that man by whom the offense cometh.' If we shall suppose that American slavery is one of those offenses which in the providence of God must needs come, but which having continued through His appointed time, He now wills to remove, and that He gives both the North and South this terrible war as the woe due to those by whom the offense came, shall we discern therein any departure from those divine attributes which the believers in a living God always ascribe to Him? Fondly do we hope, fervently do we pray, that this mighty scourge of war may pass away. Yet, if God wills that it continue until all the wealth piled up by the bondsman's two hundred and fifty years of unrequited toil shall be sunk, and until every drop of blood drawn by the lash shall be paid by another drawn with the sword, as was said three thousand years ago, so it still must be said, 'The judgments of the Lord are true and righteous altogether.' "

Because human life is bound up in a single bundle and every life involved with every other life, the whole body suffers with every sin that affects any part of the body. The righteous do suffer with the guilty. They may suffer for the guilty. "The mark of rank in nature is capacity for pain." A great, sensitive soul may suffer the more keenly for his very greatness and sensitiveness, as he carries upon himself the burden of the sin which he shares, only because he is a part of the humanity that tolerates or commits the sin. And the tragedy resultant from the sin affects all the lives bound together in the same body. So Jeremiah sees God "visiting for these things" because His covenant compels Him to act, yet suffering with the suffering of His people, because this, too, is the character of God.

Tragedy As the Natural Consequence of Sin

There is yet another qualifying factor in our understanding of Jeremiah's concept of God and the tragedy of circumstance. The prophet's apprehension of the presence of evil in God's universe is not to be equated exactly with the simple belief that the tragedy is the punitive activity of an offended Deity. A deeper understanding of Jeremiah's total concept makes it clear that although he represents the calamities of his people as the visitation of God, he is aware of a certain order in the operation of divine law. It is important, therefore, to note Jeremiah's *indirect answer* to the everlasting "why?" of life. How God "visits for these things" is a vital factor of the prophet's perception. There are times when his purpose is manifestly to impress upon his people the fact that God does visit. The records of these stirring announcements must be read in the light of other great declarations which indicate the prophet's understanding that some tragedy at least is present in God's universe because it is the natural and inevitable consequence of sin. *Acts have consequences.* This is the whole truth of Jeremiah's wrestling with the problem. And though it may not be stated with each burning declaration of the visitation of God, it is stated so often and so clearly that it sheds its light on all that the prophet says.

This truth has been examined somewhat in detail in a preceding chapter. It needs only to be reiterated here. Like Habakkuk, Jeremiah "teaches us to recognize and respect the nature of things" (W. J. Farley). There is a sequence in life. Sin brings certain evils in its train, not because a jealous Deity has decreed a proportionate retribution, but because it is inevitable in the nature of things. The moral order exists. There is an inevitability which it is salutary to recognize. Sin destroys because it is its nature to do so. Its chief punishment is the sin itself. The plainest statement of this is the oft-quoted word, "Be thy scourge thine own sin." But the truth cannot be missed in such passages as 16:10 which pictures the

188

moral obtuseness, the spiritual blindness, the warped judgment produced by sin; or 18:15, 16, in which the poetic Jeremiah sings:

> They have come to grief in their ways
>   The tracks of yore,
> Walking in paths uneven,
>   A road unpaved;
> To make their land a desolation
>   A scoff for all time.
> All who pass are shocked
>   They shake their heads.
>
> —Tr. by John Skinner

When, after the ravages of war, agents of rehabilitation visited prostrate Germany, they were appalled at the devastation. Cities which had stood for centuries were heaps of rubble. Industries developed by the best scientific ingenuity of man were twisted, broken piles of wreckage. Temples, the expression of man's noblest art, lay in ruins. These visitors thought of the arrogance, the stubborn human lust for power, that resulted in this havoc. Martin Niemoeller, addressing the students of Erlangen University early in 1946, traced the final collapse and ruin of the Reich to what he specifically called the "sin" of his people. In his own words, they had made "their highest dogma" this: "To enjoy life is the highest good." As men searched for words to describe the situation and its source, they could not have done better than repeat the speech of Jeremiah: "To make their land a desolation, a scoff for all time. All who pass are shocked; they shake their heads." *Acts have consequences!*

One of the most striking presentations of this is in Chapter 30, the essence of which is that sin leaves its mark even upon the forgiven and restored sinner. "I will correct thee in measure and in no wise leave thee unpunished" (30:11). Even in the midst of a song of rejoicing, celebrating the prospect of a healed and restored nation—"the release of hope"—there comes the minor strain as the prophet recognizes that Judah's sin has left an ineradicable mark. A merciful God may forgive and restore the offender. But like a wasting disease the sin has registered itself in the scarred tissues and fibers of the life. Joseph Jefferson's "Rip Van Winkle" was made to say, as he yielded weakly to repeated temptations, "I won't count this time." But, however he might be determined not to "count this time," his physical, mental, and moral nature perforce registered it. He could overlook; God could forgive, but life recorded the sin inevitably, and somewhere in the total complexity of his nature it was counted. The scars were left.

It is just this perception that accounts for Jeremiah's acceptance of final defeat and dismemberment as the only destiny of the nation.

And as the bad figs that cannot be eaten, they are so bad, surely thus saith Jehovah, So will I give up Zedekiah the king of Judah and his princes and the residue of Jerusalem that remain in this land . . . I will even give them up to be tossed to and fro among all the kingdoms of the earth for evil, to be a reproach, and a proverb and a taunt and a curse. . . . And I will send the sword, the famine, and the pestilence among them until they be consumed from off the land that I gave unto them and their fathers (24:8-10).

No one in his day could understand Jeremiah's strange counsel of surrender. He seemed to his people a quisling. They protested that he weakened the morale, the resistance of the men of war. Various considerations moved him to this counsel. But uppermost in his mind was his perception of the inevitable and natural consequences of sin. Acts have consequences! Bad figs cannot be eaten. There is no patching up, renewing or restoring for figs that are spoiled. Judah is a fig that has spoiled. A lover of the nation may yearn for the restoration of the good old days. He may persist in the belief that a good God will somehow restore the pristine glory of the nation and once more bless His heritage. But Jeremiah is a realist who sees that whatever man may desire, the processes of sin have been at work in the life too long. The figs are overripe, beyond recovery. Sin has written its effects irretrievably. The physical outlines of the state, the external institutions and features, must go. Surrounding nations will be the instruments for the accomplishment of the destiny. But the experience itself is the inevitable consequence of the sin to which the people have given themselves. They are "wholly intractable stuff."

Here is a perception that is exceedingly important. Where were the Ten Commandments first written? They were not written first in tablets of stone on Mt. Sinai. They were graven first in human life—written upon tablets of life before they were graven upon tablets of stone. They are what they are because life is what it is. They are not the arbitrary decrees of a jealous God—set about men to keep life in bounds—but the signposts erected by a loving Father who knows all the possibilities of the forces He has created. "In the keeping of them there is life."

St. Paul, in the letter to the Romans, bears witness to a fundamental truth when he says: "For where the Gentiles who have not the law do by nature the things of the law, these not having the law are a law unto themselves: in that they show the work of the law written in their hearts." There is a law which is a part of life itself. It existed before men, inspired or uninspired, committed it to writing. This eternal, inherent principle is what Sophocles describes in his lines in *Antigone*:

> The unwritten and unswerving laws of heaven,
> Not of today and yesterday are they,
> But from everlasting.

The solemn word of Jeremiah to the nation and to the individual is that in the violation of the fundamental law of God there is death. And for the prophet the main necessity is not to explain why tragedy comes because of sin, but to realize that it does come, and so live that ripeness and not the decay of rottenness shall be life's reward.

The Suffering Servant

Jeremiah's most valuable contribution to religious thinking on the question of the presence of tragedy in God's universe is not to be found in any specific statement or defined conclusion of his. It is rather to be seen in the whole experience and attitude of the prophet and the testimony of the ages.

There are three fundamental approaches to the problem of the tragedy that life holds. One is escape. Man's natural impulse is to avoid suffering if it is at all possible to do so. There have been those indeed who charge that this is the whole reason for his resort to religion. Religion is an "escape mechanism," a way of cushioning the shocks of life from which no other device of his can save him. Jeremiah played with the idea of escape. He put it frankly in one of his most telling verses:

192

O that I had in the desert a wayfarer's lodge
For fain would I leave this people
And go clean away (9:2).

He reiterated it in one of his laments, pouring out his regret that he had ever known the gift of life. Nonexistence was preferable to the struggle. "Cursed be the day wherein I was born: let not the day wherein my mother bore me be blessed. Cursed be the man who brought tidings to my father, saying, A man child is born unto thee; making him very glad" (20:14, 15). Any escape from the stern battle of life with its frustrations, its perplexities, its tragedies, was welcome.

Another approach to the problem is the intellectual approach. Study the question. Revolve it in the mind. Search for a satisfying answer to the question "Why?" This way, too, occupied the mind of Jeremiah. It was the implication of his question, "Righteous art thou, O Jehovah, when I contend with thee; yet would I reason the cause with thee; wherefore doth the way of the wicked prosper?" (12:1). Like every other individual Jeremiah applied the powers of his intellect to the problem. He would "reason the cause." He would bring his best faculties to bear upon life's baffling mystery and arrive at a satisfying answer.

A third way of dealing with this issue is the moral approach. Men are not limited to two alternatives in their relation to the problem of suffering: either escape or explanation. There is a third way which transcends all others, namely the acceptance and use of adversity for the victory of the soul. Any man's solution to the problem is to be seen less in what he says than in how he lives. One man may feel that he has faced this most perplexing question of life successfully if he has managed prudently to escape suffering. Another may believe that he has achieved the desideratum of life if he has been able to evolve airtight answers that are satisfying to the most inquiring intellect. A few choice spirits will find their victory neither in the fortune that furnishes escape nor in the cleverness that contrives answers, but in the will that lays hold upon every circumstance of life, friendly or hostile, and turns it to victory.

One searches in vain through the writings of Jeremiah for a neat, compact answer or set of answers to the baffling mystery of tragedy. But one finds in his spirit, his dedication, and his conduct of life a bright illumination. A first glimmer of this light appears early in his career. Disappointed because he is not a "successful" prophet—his predictions have not exactly come true, his hearers have not been won to his position, his preaching has aroused antagonism, and enemies seek his life—he is in the doldrums. He has tried and failed and is now ready to wash his hands of the whole matter. His career has come to an early and inglorious end. He is disposed to quarrel with the God whose ways he cannot understand.

Into this mood God moves dynamically and Jeremiah's attitude is revolutionized.

If thou hast run with the footmen and they have wearied thee, then how canst thou contend with horses? and though in a land of peace thou art secure, yet how wilt thou do in the pride of Jordan? (12:5).

God's way of lifting him out of the discouragement of failure is not to grant to him escape, or even to answer the questions he asks. He gives to this man, sulking because he has failed in the small task, a greater task to do. He calls him

194

from defeat in the petty things to heroic endeavor with the important things. He has run with footmen and has become wearied. Very well, he shall contend with horses. He has not done so well in the village of Anathoth. He will move on to the great city, the pride of Jordan. He will be taken away from the defeat he cannot explain and be hurled into a mightier contest in a greater arena than he has yet known. In the homely parable Jeremiah learned the first lesson of the victorious life. Lay hold upon life. Move out of the area of speculation into the area of action. Cease the effort merely to understand. Accept the responsibility to which God calls.

It is related that a student once came to Dean Hodge of Princeton Theological Seminary to seek counsel concerning some intellectual difficulties that beset him. "Dr. Hodge," he said, "I am perplexed and confused about some of the cardinal doctrines of our religion. I wish you would go over with me the arguments for the Virgin Birth, the Deity of Jesus, and the Atonement." The dean replied, "My son, what you need is not more argument but a closer touch with life. Plunge your sickle unto the harvest. Learn to know the joy of growing weary in service. Your doubts will vanish as the morning mists." That kind of lesson God taught the discouraged young prophet of Anathoth.

The lesson Jeremiah learned in that experience became the guiding star of his whole career. He gave himself wholly to God, contending powerfully for the right as God gave him to see the right. He fought the battle of righteousness with utter dedication. He contended against wickedness in high places and low. He proclaimed the word of the Lord with unflagging zeal, and identified himself with his message and with his people with a completeness seldom realized. Yet this man, wholly dedicated to God and truth, was stripped

195

of everything men cherish, defeated in the eyes of man, dishonored and humiliated. And besides the evil he suffered personally, he was compelled to see all that for which he contended going down to crushing defeat. Yet he fought his battle without compromise.

A generation which has become accustomed to setting up its standards of success and measuring values in terms of the visible and the material may find it difficult to understand Jeremiah. The president of Lafayette College, Dr. Ralph C. Hutchison, addressing the Presbyterian General Assembly in May, 1946, and pleading with the Church not to surrender the field of higher education, made some striking observations concerning the spirit of his time. "The tragedy of our day is that there is no party that would rather be true than win an election, no nation that would rather be just than be victorious, no candidate who would rather be right than president. This is the tragedy, that in the great labor struggles there is none to say, 'We will accept defeat before we will do wrong to any man.' It is a tragedy that more of the note of moral right and wrong is not heard in the arguments of our smart governmental and political economists, and less of this cynical, ruthless doctrine of expediency and devotion to success."

To the age than can be thus described Jeremiah will be a failure. "Successful" preaching in the judgment of the world means a large, approving hearing, an honored pulpit, an influential ministry. And the Church to a very large degree has fallen down and worshiped the idol of success. To be true to a great principle, to speak the truth though men turn away, to vindicate the message by dying for it, is to speak to this age in "another language." But the true prophet is measured not by the vindication of his preaching in large audiences

196

and larger collections so much as by his dedication to the truth.

Dr. Rufus Jones of Haverford once spoke a memorable word in the course of a sermon, "Great Adventures." Using as his text Moffatt's translation of Peter's speech to the Sanhedrin (Acts 3:15), "You killed the Pioneer of Life," he called upon his hearers to become the followers of this Pioneer. "The success of a great adventure," said he, "is not the praise or flattery of men, nor the reward and glory, but the adventure itself." He described the achievement of a company of explorers who ascended Mt. Everest. They were believed to have reached the summit. Watchers were sure that through their glasses they had seen them at the top. Upon the return trip some tragedy snatched so-called success from their grasp. They did not return to reap the rewards of their achievement. After a very impressive pause Dr. Jones said, "You don't have to come back from a great adventure."

Jeremiah's success lay not in coming back from a great adventure, but in following through to all that the venture of faith meant. The meaning of his religion did not lie in the escape it furnished him from the dark passages of life, nor in the satisfied atttitude of mind it gave him toward the deep mysteries of life. It lay in the power which it brought him to use the tragedy of life for the furthering of God's purpose, for the larger life of others, and for the greater victory of the soul. He belongs to a choice company of valiant spirits who have laid hold upon life with all its hardness and who have found through God that which makes them conquerors—not after the selfish pattern of men, but in the sight of God who looks not upon the outward appearance but upon the heart.

A prophet who faced the tragedy of life with the skeptic's

question upon his lips "fought his doubts and gathered strength" until he came finally to sing his song of pure faith, "though the fig tree shall not blossom and there shall be no fruit in the vine; the labor of the olive shall fail and there shall be no meat in the field; the flock shall be cut off from the fold and there shall be no herd in the stall, yet will I rejoice in the Lord, and joy in the God of my salvation, and I will walk with Him in heavenly places" (Hab. 3:17-19). The victory of that song rises above every earthly disaster. Pure fellowship with God survives the loss of every item of material prosperity.

An apostle lifted his poignant cry for relief from suffering, "For this thing (the thorn in the flesh) I besought the Lord thrice that it might depart from me." But this righteous man's prayer was destined to be unanswered as men count answers to prayer. Yet it was not really unanswered; "my grace is sufficient for thee." And this man whose plea for escape from the bitter adversity has just been denied is found singing a song of victory. "Most gladly therefore will I glory in mine infirmity that the power of Christ may rest upon me, for when I am weak then am I strong." His religion has furnished him neither an answer nor an escape. It has done something more glorious. It has made him "conqueror and more than conqueror through Christ Jesus." You don't have to come back from a great adventure!

In Dr. L. P. Jacks' book, *Religious Perplexities* (p. 40), there is an illuminating reference to the speech of Baron Von Hugel. "Christianity," says the baron, "has not explained suffering and evil; no one has done so; no one can do so. Yet it has done two things more great, more profound, and more profitable for us. From the first it has immensely widened and deepened the fact, the reality, the awful potency, the baffling mystery of sorrow, pain, sin, the things that abide with man across the ages. But Christianity has also, from the first, increased the capacity, the wondrous secret and force, which issues in a practical, living, loving transcendence, utilization, transformation of pain, sorrow, and even of sin. Christianity gave to our souls the strength and the faith to grasp life's nettle."[2]

Christianity had not yet come to give Jeremiah its "strength to grasp life's nettle." But out of his yielding to the God who finally came to men in Christ, Jeremiah found the strength of which a Christian may speak confidently. He faced every tragic circumstance of life, not understanding, sometimes protesting vehemently, fighting vigorously, seldom with a satisfied mind, but always with a surrendered will. He did not learn why the way of the wicked prospers. He never did find a lodge in the wilderness for escape from the bitter experience. But who shall say that he did not find the "strength to grasp life's nettle"?

---

[2] By permission of Harper & Bros.

Jeremiah and Religious Dynamic

"God's laws are become a Greatest Happiness Principle, a Parliamentary Expediency: the Heavens overarch us only as an Astronomical Timekeeper—in our, and old Johnson's, dialect, man has lost the *soul* out of him, and now . . . begins to find the want of it. This is verily the plague spot: center of the Social Gangrene threatening all modern things with frightful death. To him that will consider it, here is the stem with its roots and taproots, with its world-wide upas boughs, and accursed poison exudations under which the world lies writhing in atrophy and agony. You touch the focal center of all our disease, of our frightful noxology of diseases, when you lay your hand on this. There is no religion. There is no God; man has lost his soul and vainly seeks antiseptic salt. Vainly; in killing kings, in passing Reform Bills, in French Revolutions, in Manchester Insurrections, is found no remedy. The foul elephantine leprosy, alleviated for an hour, reappears in new force and desperateness next hour."[1]

An exact parallel is discernible between Carlyle's penetrating analysis of society's disease and the insight of Jeremiah as he traces Judah's fatal malady to its source and dis-

---

[1] Thomas Carlyle, *Past and Present*, Book III, *The Modern Worker* Chap. I.

closes the only real remedy. For those who have eyes to see, there is an even more striking parallel between the situations of both and that of the modern world, making the prophet indeed contemporary.

Shortly after the invasion of the Continent by the Allied forces in June, 1944, it was reported that one of the units was surprised by the capture, intact, of a certain vital port. The enemy had had ample time to mine and destroy all important installations. Yet there was no demolition. Puzzled, the engineers searched for a possible trap. They discovered that explosives had been strategically placed and properly wired. But the Nazis had been too efficient. With characteristic thoroughness they had severed all the utility connections, including the main power line from the central electric plant! When the button was pressed no power flowed. Jeremiah looked at a nation reduced to impotence because it had given attention to the outlying, circumferential points, but had cut the line connecting them with the source of all power.

The nineteenth-century critic had his own bristling way of describing the situation. "Man has lost his soul and vainly seeks antiseptic salt." Jeremiah has an equally descriptive and superlatively accurate picture:

> Two evils have my people committed,
> Me they have forsaken, a fountain of living water
> To hew for themselves cisterns—
> Broken cisterns that can hold no water.
>
> —2:13; tr. by John Skinner

FOUNTAIN OR CISTERNS?

In the darkest night of Judah's life the religion of the spirit was made to shine at its brightest through the personality and the preaching of Jeremiah. Heart religion was given one of its finest expositions in the Old Testament. The heart of the prophet's truth, the climax of his teaching, is the disclosure of his insight that true religion is a dynamic.

That this conception of religious relationship and quality was a fundamental and developing understanding is indicated by the striking figure which the prophet used to call his people away from their idols to the God of their fathers, "You have forsaken the fountain to dig for yourselves cisterns." The picture was at once illuminating to the people of that arid land. The fountain, fed from interior sources, bubbling up with fresh, clear, pure, water, meant life to thirsty animals and people, and to a sun-parched countryside, shade and vegetation. The cisterns were man-made, crumbling, leaking reservoirs. They stored water supplied from without which often became stagnant. At their best they were poor substitutes for the ever-flowing fountains of fresh water. At the well of Sychar, the Samaritan woman in her speech to Jesus testified to the gratitude and esteem in which the man was held who dug a well or made available a fountain: "Art thou greater than our father Jacob who dug this well?" And an unknown poet in his song likened the service of true religion to that of the benefactor who in the parched land crossed by pilgrim feet provided a supply of refreshing water: "Blessed is the man whose strength is in thee. . . . Passing through the valley of Baca, they make it a place of springs" (Ps. 84:5, 6). Speaking to a people whose situation made them familiar with the pitiful inadequacy of cisterns, and whose experience made the words "spring" and "fountain" the very symbols of life, Jeremiah's figure was particularly descriptive.

The interpreter must be on guard against the temptation of reading too much into this figure. It does not have a New

202

Testament content. It could not possibly have meant to Jeremiah the same thing that a similar figure meant to Jesus. The cisterns upon which he saw his nation relying were, as the earlier portion of this chapter indicates, the various deities and the man-made idols which he described as "vanities" (2:5). They were artificial, exhaustible, and shallow reservoirs of an external variable supply. Over against these vanities Jeremiah saw the Living God. He knew God as Providence (2:6, 7) a living, active Power. In the keeping of his commandments there was life. Forsaking this God for the "vanities" was like forsaking a fountain for a cistern.

It is significant that Jeremiah could think and speak of God under this figure. The poem in which it occurs belongs to the early period of his prophetic career. This indicates that the conception enshrined in it was an abiding one, not a later acquisition. It underlay all his thinking about religion and life, to give light to his interpretations and direction to all his conclusions and counsel. God was, in contrast to all the other resorts and reliances of men, like a fountain of living water. That is to say, he thought of religion as an inner quality, as that which rises like a spring from within the life. Here is a foregleam of that spiritual conception of religion which came to its finest expression in Christ, and which He Himself put in the same figure, "Whosoever drinketh of the water that I shall give him shall never thirst; but the water I shall give him shall become in him a well of water springing up unto eternal life" (John 4:14).

Jeremiah did not know God as He finally revealed Himself in Christ Jesus. But the God he knew was the same God who did reveal Himself by making His qualities incarnate in the Man who walked by Galilee. And manifestly one of the deeper truths about this God that fixed itself in his mind and heart was a truth he could describe only with the same picture that Christ later employed. Religion was for Jeremiah, as for Jesus, a well of living water springing up and flowing from within the life.

Henry Van Dyke, in "The Source,"[2] tells of a traveler who, coming to a certain town, was impressed by the community's flourishing life. Trees and shrubbery, grasses and vegetation were green and lush. Little children played happily in the parks and by the banks of a stream that flowed through the town. The clear, freshly flowing stream seemed to give a cleanness and fertility to all the life of the place. In fact, the traveler was told, the citizens believed this to be true, and in recognition of it made periodic pilgrimages to the source of the river. They felt that there was a connection between the undiminishing and life-bestowing flow of the stream and their visits to the source.

After many years the traveler returned to the community to discover that the whole aspect of its life had changed. No longer did the sparkling stream flow through the town and its surrounding fields. Hard-surfaced streets had replaced the green and flourishing grass. The shrubbery seemed withered or blighted. And the people had lost the joy, the concord, the brightness which formerly marked their life. Searching, the traveler found an old inhabitant who recalled the traditions of the former days which the newer citizens had never learned. This old man told him that people had come to regard the pilgrimage to the source as a superstition. Why depend upon so precarious a means of supply when science had now instructed men to dig artesian wells which

---

[2] In *The Blue Flower* (New York: Charles Scribner's Sons, 1902).

were more modern and dependable? So now the community no longer visited the mountain source of their stream, but relied upon the reservoirs which were more scientific and efficient.

For Jeremiah the resort of his people to the "vanities" was like the self-impoverishing stupidity of these citizens who put their trust in the works of their own hands. They were forsaking the Living Source. If he had been permitted to live in the full light of the Christian revelation he would have taken his stand by the side of St. Paul and added his voice to the apostle's plea; for his perception was of the same order: "O foolish Galatians, who did bewitch you, before whose eyes Jesus Christ was openly set forth crucified? This only would I learn from you, Received ye the Spirit by the works of the law, or by the hearing of faith? Are ye so foolish? Having begun in the Spirit, are ye now perfected in the flesh?" (Gal. 3:1-3). Religion could never be, either for Paul or Jeremiah, a merely external relationship. Each had experienced it in his own way as an inner spiritual power. Like a fountain it flowed to bestow life and fertility.

It is important to note this early conception of the religious life in the thinking of Jeremiah. For it had formative influence in the reaching of that final conviction which became the crown of his contribution to religious thought. All along, he knew God as the source, the eternal fountain, and religion as an inner spiritual power. It was natural then, when he faced the ultimate issues, for him to summarize his religious convictions in one of the Old Testament's most distinctive definitions of the religion of the Spirit. The new covenant is the logical outgrowth of Jeremiah's basic conception revealed in this early poem.

To grasp fully the extent, the depth, and the implications of Jeremiah's most profound insight it is necessary to set it against the background of his own experience. It will be recalled, as earlier chapters have noted, that the young prophet in Anathoth welcomed Josiah's reforms and aligned himself with the movement and the hopes begotten by the recovery of the Deuteronomic Code. His espousal of the reform aroused hostility in his fellow-townsmen and culminated in the plot against his life. Moving him, as it did, into the larger arena of Jerusalem, it became one of the turning points of his career.

A reformer in spirit and activity, Jeremiah's career furnishes many interesting parallels to the experiences of the sixteenth-century reformers. Bitterly disappointed in Anathoth, the young idealist came with high expectation to Jerusalem, in much the same mood, we may believe, as that in which Martin Luther came to Rome to ascend the Sancta Scala. But like Luther he found no realization of his hopes, only further disillusionment. In the same manner that Luther, supposing the hierarchy to be unaware of the abuses thriving in the provinces took measures to appeal to the heads of the church, Jeremiah turned from "the poor, the ignorant folk" to the "great ones." Like Luther again he saw that the infection had possessed all ranks of society. "Deep beyond sounding is the heart and sick beyond cure." Reform upon the circumference was not enough.

Here lies the real significance of Jeremiah's message which can be appreciated only when his position with reference to the reformation of his day is thoroughly understood. The work of the sixteenth-century reformers was made possible by a company of pre-Reformation heroes, like Huss, Savonarola, and Wycliff, who prepared the way. The paradox in Jeremiah's career is that he was not a pre-, but a post-reformation reformer.

Before the prophet came upon the scene, the reform had already been accomplished. The Social Gospel had been proclaimed in Judah. It had had its inception at the very highest level, with the king himself. Josiah gave to this reform the sanction of the nation's chief authority, and located it not upon the fringes of society, but in the very center, the temple itself.

The atmosphere in which the life of the people was expressed was the concern of the reform. It struck at the visible sources of the evil that was vitiating the life of the nation. Josiah saw clearly enough that the shrines of the idolaters and the licentious practices associated with them were a real threat to the nation's security. They must go! And in their place the temple at Jerusalem was made supreme. To complete the effectiveness and seal the authority of the whole movement, the divine sanction was given in Deuteronomy. Here were prescribed minutely and specifically the rules for every man's life and conduct. The way was charted. The outlines of a righteous and secure society were established. The reformer's paradise was set up.

And yet life was breaking up! All the successful changes of the reforming group were apparently powerless to halt the disintegration which was proceeding from within, or to avert the disaster boiling up from without. Jeremiah saw a nation living in the wake of a reform, yet moving inevitably toward its death. Augustine felt with dismay the impact of disaster when the hordes of Alaric sacked Rome, A.D. 410. He was moved by that staggering event to write his *De Civitate Deo*. From the city of man's pride, now shaken and destroyed, he turned to the eternal City of God that cannot be shaken. So did Jeremiah turn from the tottering Jerusalem to the "city that hath foundations, whose builder and maker is God." He turned from the law written upon parchment and preserved in a holy place to the law written upon the heart and preserved by the eternal covenant of God. "Out of the heart are the issues of life."

If the best society man was able to construct, even in the name of religion, was not good enough; if the most complete set of rules he could devise could not guard the life; if the most thoroughgoing reforms the best minds could accomplish were unable to produce the good life, must he then give up, frustrated? Is there nowhere in the universe a salutary power above and beyond these best instruments? Is life forever doomed to futility?

Out of reflections like these came Jeremiah's inspired declaration, whose import is as vital for the twentieth century A.D. as it was for the sixth century B.C.

Behold, the days come, saith Jehovah, that I will make a new covenant with the house of Judah: not according to the covenant that I made with their fathers in the day that I took them by the hand to lead them out of the land of Egypt; which my covenant they brake, although I was a husband unto them, saith Jehovah. But this is the covenant I will make with the house of Israel after those days, saith Jehovah: I will put my law upon their inward parts and in their heart I will write it and I will be their God and they shall be my people. And they shall teach no more every man his neighbor, saying, "Know Jehovah"; for they shall know him from the least unto the greatest of them . . . for I will forgive their iniquity, and their sin will I remember no more (31:31-34).

Beyond Deuteronomy Jeremiah found the source of the

good life. In one of his prayers he had voiced this perception: "O Jehovah, I know that the way of man is not in himself. It is not in man that walketh to direct his steps" (10:23). He had witnessed the failure of the best effort of man to direct his steps, the insufficiency of his best reforms and most complete legal controls. Now he looked beyond all these to see the source of life in God—that God whom he had long known as a fountain of living water.

Silhouetted as it is against the dark background of Deuteronomy's failure, Jeremiah's "new covenant" is seen to possess certain positive and instructive characteristics. (1) God is the initiator of this new life. The word is very strong: "I will put my law upon their hearts." The creation of the good life Jeremiah sees as the work of God. (2) It is inward and spiritual, a dynamic and not an external accomplishment. "Upon their inward parts—in their hearts will I write it." The old covenant was written upon tablets of stone. It was laid upon the life by the instruction of teachers and with the sanction of the law. The new covenant is an inner, spiritual reality. Its good life proceeds from within. (3) It is, moreover, a covenant. "I will be their God, and they shall be my people." Its effectiveness depends upon both parties. God does not miraculously confer a good life, even upon His own people, apart from the actual reality of keeping Him in deed and truth as God. (4) And this good life of the new covenant is *experienced* rather than taught. The significance of this quality cannot be overemphasized. Here in the darkest days of the Old Testament a prophet of the spirit is proclaiming a God who is known, not by word of instruction, but through His own act of the forgiveness of sins. "They shall teach no more . . . saying, 'Know Jehovah,' for they shall know him. . . . For I will forgive their iniquity." The God of the new covenant is a God who is known experientially by men whose sins are forgiven.

These characteristics give to Jeremiah's speech a peculiar relevance for contemporary life.

OUT OF THE HEART

The cisterns men have dug have varied with the passing centuries. Jeremiah saw them as "the vanities," the rival deities. He saw them also as the reliance upon externals, upon legalism and all human accomplishment. Thomas Carlyle saw them as "French Revolutions, Reform Bills, and Manchester Insurrections." The eyes of the twentieth century see them in different forms and with varied designations. But whatever their name and form may be, Jeremiah's insight is equally applicable. "It is not in man that walketh to direct his steps." The good life of man, whether of the individual or of society, is not a human accomplishment. The most complete code laid upon the life cannot bring it to pass. It must come from within. Only through the act of God writing His law upon the inward parts can life be made secure. Religion is more than behavior, more than a program of social or even religious reform. It is a dynamic.

Humanism, that is, trust in the skills, the capacities and the masteries of man, is essentially the opposite against which Jeremiah's new covenant asserts itself. The "Humanist Manifesto" contains among its theses such assertions as these: "Religious humanism considers the complete realization of human personality to be the end of life and it seeks this development in the here and now." "The quest for the good life is the central task. . . . Man alone is responsible for the fulfillment of his dreams, and he has within himself the

210

powers requisite for their achievement."[3] So say a company of writers, teachers, reformers, who would capture the thinking of the twentieth century, and whose basic assumptions have a wide acceptance. Politely, they bow God out of the universe. "The way of man is not in himself," says Jeremiah, asserting a wisdom that the records of history have served to verify.

Legalism, that is, reliance upon the external code or statute—often the chief implement of humanism—has repeatedly failed to produce the good life. Of course, humanly speaking, nothing could be more practical and explicit than this sixth-century B.C. example of this reliance. If the rules for every man's conduct can be plainly stated and decreed so that for every circumstance of life he can turn to an authoritative code and find the law, it ought to be apparent that society must be secure, and life good. But it was not, actually. The more minute and explicit the directions were, and the more multiplied they became, the more evil life grew to be. External legalistic righteousness produced the system which Jesus denounced, whose product the New Testament describes as "trusting in themselves that they were righteous." John Skinner has quoted Dr. Davidson, the British theologian, as saying, "Deuteronomy and Pharisaism came into the world on the same day."[4]

The demonstrated failure of a reform—with which he was in sympathy—to produce the good life caused Jeremiah to turn away from the laws written upon parchment to the covenant written in the heart. He perceived that which Martin Luther later understood and embodied in his "Treatise

---

[3] From "The Humanist Manifesto," in *The Christian Century*, June 7, 1933.

[4] *Prophecy and Religion*, p. 96.

on the Mass." "Experience, all chronicles, and the Holy Scriptures teach us this truth: the less law, the more justice; the fewer commandments, the more good works. No well-regulated community existed long, if at all, when there were many laws."[5]

Outward circumstances and expressions change. The principle persists. Life's final forces are always spiritual. Society's efforts to achieve the good life by devising the most enlightened, modern, and complete controls have always resulted in failure. They are like the catastrophe of the "Morro Castle." This luxury liner, carrying pleasure-bent tourists between New York City and Havana, took fire upon one of its voyages in the fall of 1934 and burned to a blackened shell with tragic loss of life. Maritime authorities had devised the most complete code for the safety of vessels. Technological advances had provided every protection—automatic fire doors and sprinklers, life boats and rafts, alarm systems and radio communications. The ship was disaster-proof. It was disaster-proof at every point except the most vital—the human spirit. Venal inspectors and officials had conspired with greedy operators to allow the maritime regulations to go unenforced. Careless navigators had permitted the fire doors to rust on their hinges, and the davits that swung the life boats to become rigid with disuse. Labor grievances had made radio operators sullen and resentful. Every modern scientific and legal safeguard was canceled by human failure, and that chiefly in the area of the spirit.

So are the best, the most enlightened human devices rendered impotent without the soul of man, empowered by

---

[5] "A Treatise on the New Testament, that is, The Holy Mass," *Works of Martin Luther* (Phila.: A. J. Holman Co.) Vol. I, p. 294.

the law within. The principle is amply illumined by history and the experience of society. The problems of human relationship may be approached from several points. Here is the question of industrial justice. One attitude will attack this problem upon the circumference: enact laws, devise codes, regiment industry. Another attitude will rely not primarily upon safeguarding laws, but will endeavor to reach the hearts of men, knowing that only when men have the love of God, of justice and their fellow-men, in their hearts is any order safe. Here is the problem of international peace. One attitude will resolve the problem by setting up conferences, writing pacts, organizing leagues. Another, knowing that— when any powerful group wills war—treaties become only scraps of paper, will labor unceasingly to change the hearts of men. Its holders will see no less acutely the denial of Christianity inherent in the institution of warfare, and demand no less sternly that it be replaced by a more enlightened, Christlike instrument. But they will be aware, too, of that which Dr. George Buttrick so well states: "We are prepared to slay the enemy. Here is the truth: The only possible defense is in the mind and means that will slay the enmity."[6] They will be impressed by current history's record of the failure of the external law and human devices. Their chief pilgrimage will be not to Geneva, Paris, San Francisco, or a United Nations capital, but to Bethlehem, and thence to Calvary. They will know that the saving hope of society is not in writing pacts, or promoting platforms, but in the covenant of God written upon the hearts of men.

Religion is always in danger of going back to those very "beggarly elements of the law" whose failure Jeremiah began

---

[6] *The Christian Fact and Modern Doubt* (New York: Charles Scribner's Sons), p. 59.

to see, which cried out for Christ and His redemptive work, and which the apostles recognized as the antithesis of the genius of their religion. "Our sufficiency is of God," said St. Paul, resorting to the very language of Jeremiah, "who also made us sufficient as ministers of a new covenant, not of the letter but of the spirit; for the letter killeth, but the Spirit giveth life." Religion may easily be thought of as zeal for a social program. It is, as Jeremiah so long ago perceived, *zeal for God*, created and sustained by the soul's fellowship with Him. And from this relation to God, as water from a living fountain, flows the good life of the citizen of this world.

The truth which Jeremiah saw so clearly and which turned his eyes toward the new covenant is that law depends for its effectiveness upon the spirit to obey. St. Paul put it, "What the law could not do in that it was weak through the flesh." All law is weak through the flesh. The situation of society today is possibly the most vivid example the world has had of the ineffectiveness of a merely legal external control without the spirit.

Consider as symptomatic of a common approach to life's adjustments an experiment once conducted by Walter B. Pitkin, which he called "Grading The Ten Commandments." Prompted by criticisms of conventional morality that he had heard, he invited a group of more than a hundred educators, social workers, and students to participate in his experiment. They were asked to indicate what in their opinion is the relative importance of the Commandments. Their replies were tabulated, and if the consensus opinion of these people had written the Ten Commandments in the order of their importance to them, the first would be "Thou shalt not kill," the second, "Honor thy father and thy mother," and the sixth, "Thou shalt have no other gods before me."

214

Here is an indication of that approach which begins not with the enthronement of God, but with social adjustments. Human relationships are thrust into the foreground. The relationship to the Divine is pushed into the background. Social maladjustments are apparent, and defeat the goal of the good life. Murder, theft, adultery, to use the ideas of the Commandments; social injustice, industrial oppression, dishonest administration, to use modern terms, are the enemies of the realization of life's best possibilities. These must be dealt with by addressing our efforts to them. The first and important duty is to abolish from our life these manifest evils. And in the sixth place on our program, to be chosen or rejected, as a sort of elective in life's curriculum, may come the relation to God.

There is more involved here than an isolated experiment. This is modern man saying, "The way of man is in himself." It is an epitome of society's way of pursuing the goal of the good life. The major emphasis in social practice and in much of our educational program has long been applied at just this point. At the same time that men are making the sixth commandment first and allowing the first to slip back into sixth place, the very evils they would eliminate and upon which they focus their efforts grow steadily worse. Murder, theft, adultery are increasing in alarming progression. So pronounced is the failure to control them by external restraints imposed upon the life that one is moved to ask whether there is not here a definite instance of cause and effect. Has a modern enlightened society been guilty of crooked thinking? The disastrous fact is only too plainly apparent. We have been saying by our programs, our platforms, and our emphases that the first commandment is "Thou shalt not kill" and the sixth is "Thou shalt honor God," with the result that neither is God honored nor murder abated.

Seldom have men of good intention given so much thought and energy to the planning of a good society, and the enactment of the laws to realize it. Never were the citizens, at least of the United States, surrounded by so many laws. And yet lawlessness was never more rampant than it is today. One nobly conceived reform after another has failed. The tragedy is that most of the reforms deserved to succeed. Failure has come, not at the point of the enabling and safeguarding laws, but at the point of the human spirit. Modern life with its confusion in spite of law has demonstrated the impossibility of building the "beloved community" apart from the spirit of love in the citizens of the community. Forgetful of the fact which Mr. Spencer noted that "You cannot make the golden age out of leaden instincts," society has gone on trying to bring in the golden age without regard to the quality of the instincts of those who compose it.

Raymond Robbins, social leader and reformer, once told of a significant experience he had had in Germany. It was shortly before the outbreak of the first phase of the World War in 1914. He was visiting the universities, lecturing and conferring informally with the students. He said they listened attentively and respectfully as he spoke of various phases of life in the United States. They were absorbingly interested in the social institutions and customs of this country, in its industrial life and educational methods, its governmental and economic order. But when he began to speak of religion they showed signs of impatience. Finally one youth voiced what was manifestly the mind of the group. "Mr. Robbins," he said, "we of the educated classes in this country are not greatly interested in religion, save as a phenomenon of his-

216

tory. We look upon it as outmoded, belonging to an age of superstition. Besides," he added, "if society is to be lifted and a good life achieved, it will not be by religion but by *Kultur*." Scarcely had the echoes of that speech died away than the world was plunged into a whirlpool of destruction in which every one of civilization's most vaunted masteries was employed as a weapon that well-nigh destroyed its own creators.

The underlying assumption of the German youth's speech, not so blatantly declared, is enshrined in the "Humanist Manifesto." It has been widely accepted and practically employed in the building of our world. A striking visual exhibit of it was "The World of Tomorrow," New York's ambitious fair of the late 1930's. There human genius outdid itself devising a countryside and cities—a world in which considerations of speed, safety, transportation, commerce, education, amusement, completely overshadowed the temple of religion. In the "shape of things to come" the spire of the church was scarcely discernible. An impressive world the genius of man devised. It was scientific achievement at its incredible utmost. The effect of its dazzling accomplishments was to say "man has within himself the powers requisite for the realization of his dreams." "If the good life is to be achieved it will be not by religion but by *Kultur*." Here was the scale model of that kind of world.

A visitor to "The World of Tomorrow," late in 1939, was tremendously impressed by the works of men's minds and hands, and almost persuaded that at last scientific genius has proved that the way of man is in himself. But presently he observed that a portion of the theme building's surface had crumbled away, revealing a flimsy structure of lath and plaster beneath. It seemed like a symbol of the far more realistic crumbling then going on in the world of today. The visitor looked with melancholy interest at the Polish exhibit, with its great grill of gilded steel, symbol—so the literature said—of strength and permanence. He reflected that already the might of Poland had crumbled before the force of the invader and the nation was being dismembered, possibly never again to exist as an autonomous state. Other nations, represented by proud exhibits calculated to proclaim their might and wealth and the riches of their achievements, were being severely shaken. Over it all there seemed to hover the wraith of an ancient emperor who looked about him at the magnificence of his empire and exclaimed, "Is not this mighty Babylon which I have builded?" The next generation saw the handwriting on the wall, "Thou art weighed in the balance and found wanting." All the achievements of the "mighty Babylon" could not redeem the failure of the "thou."

Every "world of tomorrow" must concern itself with the worlds of yesterday and the vital truths they have to transmit. *Kultur*, that is, human excellence, scientific mastery, has never in history succeeded in building the good life. From the earliest records to the latest, one testimony is apparent. The nations and the civilizations so builded have been shaken. And as the masteries of man have increased and the inventions of his genius multiplied, his plight has become more desperate. Each new dazzling device is one more instrument in his hands. Its potentialities for good are matched by its potentiality for evil. How it shall be used depends wholly upon the spirit that is within man.

No one is more clear in his perception of this truth, or more urgent in declaring the need for the interior control of the spirit, than the man who professes to speak, not in the

218

name of religion but in the name of science today. With one accord the scientists, whose research has placed in the hands of man his most recent and most powerful instrument, are calling for an increase of the moral and spiritual force which alone can keep him from using his new power for his own complete destruction. Their deep concern is not now the mind that can devise but the spirit that wields every device. The march of time has brought mankind face to face with the truth that Jeremiah declared, "The way of man is not in himself."

In his poem, "Faith," George Santayana speaks of "the soul's invincible surmise." Jeremiah's leap of faith, his "soul's invincible surmise," carried him very close to the heart of a New Testament conception of religion. His new covenant is one of the loftiest peaks of Old Testament revelation. One who analyzes its entire content and marks its several features misses really but one element of the Christian fact. Christ is missing. Jeremiah, unsatisfied by the best that man could achieve, aware of "what the law could not do," looked into the future and saw a day when God would write a new covenant upon the heart of man. He did not see the Christ whose sacrificial death sealed this new covenant. But he did see its essential terms. To a certain point his perception was identical with that of St. Paul. The apostle could say, looking at one period of his life, "A Pharisee of the Pharisees, touching the righteousness of the law, blameless" (Phil. 3:5, 6). But even that estate of blameless obedience to the law could not satisfy him. He cried out, as he thought of it, "O wretched man that I am, who shall deliver me out of the body of this death?" (Rom. 7:25). To this point the prophet and the apostle were identical in outlook. Paul, however, found a positive and specific answer for his conflict. He had

219

the advantage of living "in the latter days," after "God spake through His Son." And through a deep and actual experience of Christ within his life—"I live, yet not I, it is Christ Jesus who liveth in me"—he was able to end his speech not with the despairing question, but with a triumphant declaration, "I thank God through Jesus Christ my Lord."

Jeremiah saw this afar off. When Helen Keller, liberated from her imprisoning infirmities, was told of God, it is said that her response was, "I have always known Him, but I never knew His name." The prophet apprehended the Christian truth in similar manner. His profound insight made him aware of the need for that which was beyond the best his society knew. It acquainted him with the qualities of that which God would one day supply. He described it all faithfully. But the name of Him through whom it became reality he did not yet know.

Whether or not Jeremiah's new covenant was a reasoned and deliberate prediction of Christ may be debatable. The fact is not debatable that, when Christ came, He became "the Mediator of a new covenant" which was the complete fulfillment of all that Jeremiah described. Its initiator was God. "The grace of God hath appeared bringing salvation to all men." It was inward in character, "written upon the heart." It was a *new* covenant. And its supreme purpose was that all, from the least unto the greatest, should know God, and know Him with the knowledge of experience gained through the forgiveness of sins.

The student of Jeremiah cannot fail to be impressed by the manner in which his insights, the great surmises of his soul, lift him out of his own time and unite him in spirit with the "communion of the saints." To a man who with his fellows had been "grading the Ten Commandments"—"which

220

is the first and great commandment of the law?"—Jesus replied in the very word of Deuteronomy which its reformers forgot and forsook! "The first and great commandment has to do not with behavior but heart direction. Thou shalt love the Lord with all thy heart." Speaking to an age that vainly sought by applying laws to cure the evils of life, Jeremiah said, "I will write my law upon their hearts." To a woman who thought of religion in terms of the externals of place and ceremony, Jesus spoke of the "well of water within the life, springing up unto everlasting life." To an age relying upon its manmade, crumbling cisterns, constantly needing to be patched up, and holding stagnant water, Jeremiah spoke of God as the "Living Fountain of Water." This great soul who thus knew God, and was able to speak of religion as an inner spiritual force, cannot be limited to the Old Testament. He must be considered as marching down through the centuries, seeing afar off the day of Christ the Redeemer and rejoicing in it. In spirit he belongs to the glorious company of the apostles, as well as to the goodly fellowship of the prophets. In eternity he hears the hymn of a Christian saint like Bernard of Clairvaux, and out of the depths of his soul he adds his own fervent and sincere "Amen."

> Jesus, Thou Joy of loving hearts!
> Thou Fount of life! Thou Light of men!
> From the best bliss that earth imparts
> We turn unfilled to Thee again.